TAPESTRIES OF FAITH

BLACK SGLBT STORIES OF TRIUMPH, FAMILY, LOVE & HEALING

AUTHORED BY

THE HEALERS:
A GLOVER LANE PRESS COLLECTIVE

EDITED BY

JEFFREY KING, IFALADE TASHIA ASANTI
&
AZAAN KAMAU

COVER BY
AZAAN KAMAU

Glover Lane Press
A Division of Azaan Kamau Media
4570 Van Nuys Blvd Suite 573
Sherman Oaks, CA 91403

Editor: Jeffrey King
Editor: Ifalade Ta'Shia Asanti
Editor: Azaan Kamau
Interior Design: Ifalade Ta'Shia Asanti
Book Cover Design: Azaan Kamau

First Published by Glover Lane Press June 2011

For information on book signings, bulk orders, or press info contact:
gloverlane@gmail.com or azaankamau@gmail.com

For titles by Glover Lane Press please visit:
www.gloverlanepress.webs.com

ISBN-13: 978-0615497631 (Glover Lane Press)

ISBN-10: 0615497632

The Mission of Glover Lane Press is to Uplift, Empower and Elevate the Masses

<u>Disclaimer</u>

The opinions expressed by the authors in this book are not necessarily a reflection of the publisher, editors or its subsidiaries. In honor of censor-free expression we have kept the work exactly as it was submitted give or take a few edits for clarity and conciseness. The contributions printed and published in Tapestries of Faith are done so with the permission of the writers. Writers maintain full ownership of their work.

DEDICATIONS-JEFFREY KING

God's love transcends all. I am grateful for two amazing parent who I lost very early in my life that showed me unconditional love. I am grateful to the bold LGBT people both past and present who taught me by example how to stand up in my own truth. Thank you, Rev. Carl Bean of Unity Fellowship of Christ Church for standing on the front lines for our people. Thank you, Rev. Jenenne Macklin of Living In The Light Ministry for guiding our community into the light. Thank you, Rev Michael Bernard Beckwith of Agape Spiritual Center for providing a place for all people. To the Brothers of In The Meantime, thank You for sharing this amazing journey of life. A special thanks to Jewel Thais Williams for holding us all together. I love you just the way you are.

DEDICATIONS-IFALADE TASHIA ASANTI

I give thanks to the ancestors, Orisa and Orunmila who guide and protect my life. I give thanks to my mother, Florence (RIP) for loving me regardless. I give thanks for my Aunt Janice (RIP) who was the first person I told. I give thanks for my brother, Francis, who is still my big brother! I send deep volcanic love to my wife, best friend, cheering section and divine kindred, Pepper, for her unwavering love and support of all my dreams. I also thank Cleo Manago for teaching me that I could be my fierce BLACK self and love just like I love and Lovey Curry for taking me home i.e. to my first Gay Club, the Catch One. I thank Jeffrey King for believing in me as the channel to bring this project to fruition. I thank Azaan Kamau for her love, friendship & support for over 20 years and for saying YES to this book. Finally, I thank the writers for this anthology and you the readers. Without you there would be no fabric and therefore no *Tapestries of Faith.*

DEDICATIONS-AZAAN KAMAU

I dedicate this work of healing art to all of the SGLBT African Americans who have needlessly suffered due to the ignorance of hate and homophobia. I have so much gratitude to those who empower me, it would wrap around the Earth several times! I would like to thank *all* my ancestors who have paved the road for me. I would like to thank my teachers, mentors, and friends; The Seer Ifalade Ta'Shia Asanti, The Sagacious Linda Hobbs, The Shaman Jenenne Macklin, The Mystic Michael B. Beckwith, and The Incomparable Madlyn F. Glover. I would also like to thank every *Healer* who stepped forth to bless the pages of this amazing book! I thank you!

FOREWORD-JEFFREY KING

We rise from the fertile earth and centuries of complex struggle of African, American, Gay, Lesbian, SGL, Bi and Trans. Today we stand facing the rising sun of a new day when the dreams of the slave and fight of Bayard Rustin and others not visible now manifest in the visibility of men and women bold and Black and gay, and lesbian, and SGL and bi and trans and any other labels or the absence thereof.

I am PROUD to be among the ranks of men and women who stand front and center embracing their authentic identity. So thick and rich that words can barely capture the true essence of who and what we really are and are becoming more of.

I stand on the platform with fist raised, daring to be more of me than I could have ever dreamed of as a fifteen-year-old boy attracted to both masculine and feminine energy. Today I live and love as a proud Black gay man.

Congratulations to those who have contributed to this body of work and to those who will contribute to future volumes. Know that your lives expressed and shared are a testimony to the brilliance and resiliency of Black people everywhere.

It is through your expression that a young man, woman or child will rise up and live out of the true meaning of his or her purpose, bold and spirited.

It is through your expression that a young King or Queen will put down the crack pipe, the bottle, the needle and take on life as a fulltime experience, giving everything to live at maximum capacity.

Know that your journey expressed is a gift to someone who is standing where you were. Your experience and wisdom now becomes the road map to freedom for someone wandering in the dark.

May God continue to shine light on these precious *Tapestries of Faith: Black SGLBT Stories of Triumph, Family, Love & Healing...*.

Jeffrey King is a Community Mobilizer, HIV/AIDS Activist, Founder and Executive Director of In The Meantime Men's Group, Inc. an 11 year old, 501c3 non-profit Community Service Organization that focuses on the mental, physical, spiritual and emotional Wellbeing of Black gay, same gender loving and bisexual men in Los Angeles County.

FOREWORD

IFALADE TASHIA ASANTI

I wanted Sandra, Cleo or Jewel to write this foreword. I tracked them down, hounded them, but could not sync it up. I finally surrendered to what Spirit was saying once again. Write your words, Ta'Shia. Just write your words....

Tapestries of Faith was born from a community dialogue that took place at Jewel's Catch One after a round table discussion about the movie *For Colored Girls,* in November of 2010. The event was hosted by In the Meantime Men and facilitated by myself & Rev. Freda Lanoix. I will never forget the pain or the resilience in that room. There was much reflection on the fact that while Tyler Perry's movie was one of the most accurate screen depictions of the challenges faced by Black women and Black SGL men, the beauty, power and talent of Black SGLBT people was not captured. We accepted what we already knew, if we wanted the world to know the rich fullness of our life expressions, we would have to present it ourselves.

When Jeffrey King announced to the group that an anthology would be a great start to this task and charged me with getting it done, I gasped for just a minute. But knowing how Spirit moves in and through my friend Jeffrey I accepted the task and got busy making it happen. Azaan Kamau, publisher and editor-in-chief of Glover Lane Press graciously agreed to part the seas of her overwhelming schedule to publish this anthology. Some seven months later, we give you, Tapestries of Faith....

The voices in this anthology represent a wide variety of ages, cultural and gender identities and expressions of Blackness. In reviewing the many submissions we received from across the globe, I was moved, sometimes to tears. Subsequently, I was also tickled pink that we Black SGLBT folks are some of the baddest, most prolific writers, poets and story tellers in the world. May the powerful fabric of this anthology reach, teach, heal, uplift, inspire and empower all who read it. To those who would seek to silence these voices, this is to let you know, we are and have always been here and we aren't going anywhere. You might as well love us because the bottom line is, WE ARE YOU. Fierce. Black. Fabulous. Same Gender Loving. Our history will never be erased. Ifalade Ta'Shia Asanti-Iyanifa, Orisa Priestess, Poet, Journalist & Author.

INTRODUCTION-AZAAN KAMAU

During slavery, SGLBT African's were stolen, enslaved and sold right along with their heterosexual counterparts. Our language, the way we love, our beliefs, customs and religion were replaced with something outside of ourselves. We too were stripped of everything, including our lovers and family members!

Though some Pan Africanists and Black Nationalists condemn our very existence, in pre-colonial Africa, same gender love was the norm in more than 30 African nations. These well-meaning individuals claim their hate is based in a desire to uplift and normalize the Black community yet their efforts have not strengthened us-- instead these efforts have created social barriers that've further separated SGLBT African Americans from their straight counterparts. The fact is, African society not only embraced same sex marriage, in Yoruba, Lovedu and Zulu culture, it was a part of the fabric of their traditional societies. It was part of their tapestry. We were never exiled, shamed, jailed or put to death for expressing love until Western societal views permeated African culture.

Hiding behind the cloak of religion, Black conservatives have tried to convince us that we are an abomination. Discrimination in legislation prevails as we try to protect what we have built and those we love from the perils of ignorance and homophobia. If it were not for prejudiced and slanted politics, we would not be mourning the deaths of those who were murdered by someone's hate. If it were not for big money churches spewing hate fueled anti-African rhetoric we would not be grieving the deaths of millions who died from HIV/AIDS. If our nation took a stand to fight for our SGLBT youth, the youth would not feel suicide was an option! We would not be burying them either.

After hundreds of years of slavery, conditioning and forced assimilation, SGLBT people of African descent have not only healed, we have taken back our power! Tapestries of Faith is a book about these people--a group of people who are a stable and viable part of the Black community. And it is this community who speaks on the pages of this anthology, further empowering themselves with words and stories of healing.

SGLBT African Americans endure the ultimate duality. We face the tribulations of being Black and Gay all at the same time. Though we live in the harsh realities of two worlds, it is that very experience, in my opinion, that places us among the most powerful people on the planet! No matter how many of us were slain, humiliated, cast out, raped and exiled, we have continued to exist and shine through our collective work. We are the healers, the griots, shamans and Gatekeepers. We will not be cast aside. We have the right to exist whether society accepts it or not.

We are healed.
We take back our power!

Azaan Kamau-Editor-in-Chief-Glover Lane Publishing

THE BLACK LGBT MANIFESTO: INVISIBLE NO MORE

Co-authored by Jeffrey King and edited by Stanley Bennett Clay

In the midst of so much positive change and continued challenges, a universal celebration is truly and aptly underway. The banquet has begun and the abundance of nourishment and libation fill the table to overflowing. Revelers of every sort sit side by side as brothers and sisters, husbands and wives, parents and children, co-workers and cohorts, old and new friends, former foes and the newly freed, black and white, brown and yellow, gay and lesbian, bi and trans.

But the monolithic viewpoint of who the LGBT community is belies the realities of, not only its vast nuances, but of its mighty parts that are separate, cooperating and vitally self-identified communities within the larger community, within the American community.

One such separate, cooperating and vitally self-identified community is the Black LGBT Community.

Black invisibility in America is slowly but surely becoming a thing of the past, due greatly to self-motivation and achievement against sometimes-insurmountable odds and the generous efforts of non-black friends, supporters, and visionaries.

In every aspect of American life, African Americans have climbed to the mountaintop, assessed the rich valleys, and have employed their extraordinary

12

skills, cunning, intellect, talent, and survival gifts to farm the land of opportunity and achieve greatness in record time. Few ethnic communities have risen from slavery to leadership as quickly as America's Black community.

And yet, the Black LGBT Community, that separate, cooperating and vitally self-identified community within the larger community, has been seen as unseen by so many, condescended and regulated to second-chair status at the banquet table, part of us seated behind the mainstream LGBT community, part of us seated behind the mainstream African American community, part of us sharing second place seating behind both. We sit invisible behind the gilded fan chairs of two communities we love, honor and respect, and yet are often frustrated by.

But make no mistake. We are fully aware that it is the combination of mainstream condescension and certainly our own slow action and lack of assertiveness that is the culprit of our dilemma, our invisibility.

Well we, the Los Angeles Black LGBT Community, are invisible no more! From this day forward we, as a united front, shall use our political, social, cultural, spiritual, and financial arsenal to have our voices heard, our rights respected, and our lives lived happily and freely.

From this day forward, we claim a front seat at the banquet table where who we are, what we are, and how we live and love will be an equal part of the dinner conversation.

From this day forward, you will get to know us as ordinary Americans fighting extraordinary discrimination with the fierceness of Bayard Rustin, Sojourner Truth, and Martin Luther King, Jr.

From this day forward, we will educate you with regards to our rich history, dating back to pre-colonial Africa, when we were the highly respected tribal gatekeepers. From this day forward, you will learn of our families, and come to understand that they are no different from yours.

From this day forward, we will make you aware of our black gay youth, disproportionately exposed to parental rejection, racism, gay bashing, murder, poverty, drug-use, HIV/AIDS, and teenage suicide. From this day forward, we boldly reject separate-but-equal treatment and vigorously demand constitutional protection from the tyranny of the majority when it comes to marriage.

From this day forward, we will scrutinize our political leaders, media and churches with greater discrimination, and spend our black gay dollars with greater prudence. From this day forward, we officially declare our community as a visible and vital community in America, and indeed the world.

And so on this day, we, the Los Angeles Black LGBT Community, officially declare ourselves a force to be reckoned with, feasting upon the delicacies of America's great promise, conversing, debating and negotiating on an equal basis, even as we break bread, drink the wine of our great nation's prosperity and goodness, share laughter and tears and the spoils of our collective hard work, full citizens in this great nation, seen and heard, and INVISBLE NO MORE.

The Healers

1. Jair the Literary Masturbator
2. Clay Turner
3. Kaution
4. D.R.E.D. MLDRED GERESTANT
5. Iyanifa Oyade Queen Hollins
6. Bridget (Bey) Celeste
7. Spear Collins
8. Kathy Fuller
9. Candace Ebone Mealy
10. Dale Madison
11. Shaashawn Dial
12. Ennis Jackson
13. David Payne
14. Tammy Young
15. Obie Ford III, Ph.D.
16. J. Nathan Price
17. David Jones
18. Salima MaSud
19. Bill Allen, Jr
20. Claudia Moss
21. Robin G. White
22. Renair Amin
23. Cole E. Thomas (AGenda Benda Justice)
24. Dee Renee Smith
25. Gale Sky Edeawo
26. Katrina Arango
27. Ifalade Ta'Shia Asanti
28. Marci Acoma Halili
29. C. Jerome Woods

JAIR THE

LITERARY

MASTERBATOR

And I Know Somebody Hear Him [Listen for David Kato]

...and I know somebody heard him as they bludgeoned him with a hammer [Listen for David Kato]
Blood spurting from his body
Bones Breaking
Organs collapsing
His screams silenced by ignorance and fear [Listen for David Kato]
His cries for help muffled by the cloak of Christian colonialism[Listen for David Kato]
....and I know somebody heard him as he said, "I fear for my life" when they posted his name and image in the, "Rolling Stone" with the admonishment to, "hang them"
His voice fell on deaf ears [Listen for David Kato]
His death represents a dearth of compassion and unconditional love in a time when those should be valued more than diamonds and gold
...and I know somebody heard him as he joins the ancestors [Listen for David Kato]
The countless, nameless, faceless two-spirited beings that guide us and offers peace that passes all understanding
Safe from the harassment of government and those who claim a Christ that spreads a message of hate
Do you hear him? [Listen for David Kato]
I hear him
In the wind and rain
In the still small voice in my heart that says, "go on..."
Listen for David Kato, and all the others
Speak their names
Make their lives eternal & everlasting
We are all witnesses...
Now it's time to testify....

Poem-IN THE STILLNESS

In the stillness

I wait, I ponder
Life
All it's twists and turns
I search my soul with many questions,

...Unanswered

I connect to the source of all that is and has always been

I don't need rescue
I am not lost
I don't need deliverance
I have already arrived
I desire assurance
For in times like these
My faith wavers....

Into Gardens of Delightful Mysticisms

I am cultivating my thoughts, wishes, and hopes into plants,
flowers, and foliage that will herald the springtime in my
psyche
I will no longer cast seeds of negativity in my lush, fertile mind
and produce crops that will not nourish
I will not allow the weeds of deception to sprout and take root
in my spirit, though they have their purpose, they will be cast
away
I recognize the value of manure to aid in the harvest of my
soul; the smell though not pleasant will help me mature
In glorious days of sun and a new season it is time to celebrate
that which is uniquely mine and abide abundantly in a place
where everyone and everything is welcome to enter into
gardens of delightful mysticisms
Come, sit, rest, and contemplate in this garden
Reflect on that which has gotten you to this place

Now is the time to gather your provisions and nurture your garden planted in the fullness of time

CLAY

TURNER

LOVE-CLAY TURNER

the golden glow in a ray of sun
a shadow of energy in blue sky
the calm of streams forever baptizing earth
a celebration of leaves painting the clouds
a valley of highs and a mountain of lows
hiding behind the expression on the faces of
delicate flowers
beautiful in a cavern suspended in time
the hottest of winters and the coolest of summers
discovering spring as it searches for the fall
breathing light into the midnight of a tranquil forest of high
noons
drifting while lying still in the wilderness of motion
living God
the purity of tumbling white rivers
hearing the blackness of silence
and drifting
away from complexity into this thing called...

Rainbow Colored Cocktails

dancing through the lilies as righteous colors of pastel
shorts and mauve colored glasses fill dark space
peering through an open door in search of armor for the
night's battle
the dragons of some lost mythical day find refuge in their
dungeons
a mirage of phallic images searching for reparations
lost in a furious pounding of sound in a ritualistic nightly
worship
the piercing stare or intentional glance
crystal tinged conversations caught up in puffs of white
smoke
laughter drowned within so many pieces of crushed ice into
a dry martini
ink soiling the corners of crinkled napkins written in codes
to the unknown
different shades of wet skin on ecstasy's fertile ground
like idols to their kindred that have passed on
footsteps on sweat-stained carpet
memories trapped within the grooves of old disco records
and the sticky sweetness lurks blessed by the cocktail,
cock-tales, and more cocktails
the scent of freshly tainted cologne escapes into the
atmosphere
as a rainbow drenched flag covers the entrance
it waves goodbye to yesterday's plight
a rebirth...as the world seems to sleep
and the light creeps back into plain sight
as the darkness walks proudly behind closeted doors
....searching for what it will wear on tomorrow night!!!

Passing Of Beautiful Memories

My memories told...
she loved the history in seasoned faces
lines of aged memories
eyes with withered grey visions
expectations of ancient heart
she told me that I was beautiful
symmetry of the wonderful lines of life
seed in the fruit she came to bear
growth of spirit she felt at rest
My adoration of ancestry drowned in sepia,
she allowed my tears to lie upon her covered breast
graceful flower of withered answers
she gave voice to my heritage through story and sound,
legacy
My memories told...
flowered arms would come to shelter me
delicate, leaves from the southern dogwoods
peaceful as liquid
stately elegance on still wings, forever

KAUTION

Essay-Remembering when I use to be a real attractive girl

I stood with my back to those in attendance as I looked down into my father's casket. Thoughts running through my mind—'Daddy was I good daughter?' and 'Daddy did I make you proud of me?' were companions to that one question one asks themselves, "Why?"

A few family members would come to the casket and touch my arm offering their condolences. Dutifully I acknowledge them; in a few minutes I would read his obituary and give my part of his Eulogy to send my father "home".

On that early first day of spring—his birthday to be exact, I stood before friends, my family many who were just a distant memory to me and my co workers who came to show their respect as I spoke about my father and about my family—his family whom he loved.

It was a good service. My mother told me he would have been proud. This was all I needed. At times I would feel the stares of people but shrugged it off as being family remembering me when I was still in pampers, with a head full of kinky nappy hair and rolls of baby fat stumbling along taking my first baby steps.

It didn't bother me the stares, I was use to it from people trying to figure out if I was male or female. On that day my dress revealed nothing and by outward appearances I looked like a young professional at a solemn gathering.

As I stood thanking those who attended as they left I could hear the quiet voices; the whispers that was not meant for me to hear.

"She looks like her father, that girl was always his shadow..." Sounds of, "mmmhmm" was the answer that came in all knowing tones.

"She was always a tomboy. Gone went out there and got herself a white girl."

"What white girl?'

"Don't ya see that big, tall ass white girl over there beside her mother?"

"She use to be a real attractive girl..."

I took a deep breath. "Thank you for coming..." I continued. I glanced at my reflection in the door at my short curly hair and stylist pants suit I was wearing; my eyes looking through wired framed glasses.

"She must be the man in the relationship..."

I watched as they had to escort my older brother out consoling him. Without a word I went to him and held him and felt his shoulders slump. I was his younger sister. That was all that mattered in that place and time. Our eyes locked; he looked like my father and I wondered did it matter to my brother that I loved another woman and did it matter that my long hair was gone, that I didn't wear skirts and heels and that I no longer looked like the pretty young woman that the others spoke of?

"She was always so bright in school..."

As if my sexual orientation would stop me from being a smart person, or a proud taxpaying citizen?

And I asked myself would my father love me less because I no longer looked like a girl/woman or would he hate me because I'd took testosterone?

I let my brother go and spoke to my oldest brother briefly leaving them there to talk before making my way through more family members offering condolences; swallowing down the anger building within me. In my mind today was a day for us to say good-bye and remember my father's life not hold open discussions about who appeared to be the "man" in my same gender loving relationship.

My dad had many flaws but he loved me regardless; and my mother has loved me regardless.

Their love gave me the strength to accept who I am today without shame, resentment, anger and confusion. I am transgendered; this is a part of who I am. To me and to him I would always be his first born daughter, I would always be daddy's little girl.

For a brief second I doubted myself; my choices—who I had become; who I was at that point in time. I had always prided myself on the fact I have lived my life without shame, resentment, anger and confusion and never in my life have I felt like I had to hide who I was like a dirty little secret.

I looked over to where I see them watching--the part of my family from my father's side. I was a stranger to them the adult I had become; a curiosity. Granted, I had lived my life without shame, resentment, anger and confusion but my life did not come without challenges.

I turned from them. 'Forgive them daddy for they do not even know what they do.' I breathed deeply hoping the anger would float away with the air that I had breathed and walked back inside to view my father before we made the ride to the crematorium.

Holding my mother's hand I walked by them head high, back straight, eyes clear and focused.

This was my father's birthday and the day we were laying him to rest. Their opinions, didn't matter—no amount of whispering, pointing and shaking of their heads as if I was something to pity would change the fact my father left this earth lovingly accepting who I was as a person.

Both he and my mother gave me a wonderful gift that I have treasured throughout my life—the gift to accept and love myself fully.

It was my parents love for me that had throughout the years sustained me when life was hard and the road to self discovery and personal love of myself was tested.
'She looka like a man…' I found myself thinking in the voice of the oriental character from Mad TV, Mrs. Swan causing me to smile for the first time that day and my mother to ask me why I was grinning.

"I'm smiling because dad would want me to." I answered. I knew it would be alright.

D.R.E.D.

MILDRED GERESTANT

From her one Womb-Man show "D.R.E.D.: Daring Reality Every Day" / "When She Was King" © 1995 to 2011

"Who do you choose to experience? Woman? Man? Both? Neither? What makes a boy? What makes a girl? Is it about the clothes you wear? Your body? Your movements? What if we were free from birth to express ourselves the way we want? Without our gender expression – or any other expression - being chosen for us before we are even born? What kind of world will that be? Well I, DRED aka MilDred Gerestant, am here to create that world with you.

My inner male character D.R.E.D. makes me feel like a natural woman. In the beginning of my career as DRED, I went out in public disguised as a man many times. As a man in society I felt more comfortable taking up my own space, I felt safer walking alone late at night, and I didn't worry about how I looked – but it bothered me that I didn't feel these same things as my woman self. I found out that embracing the male energy in me empowers my woman self. Each time I bite my apple that I pull from my crotch I reclaim my power as a woman, as a human being, as a spiritual being - taking away power from that Adam and Eve story that has cause needless suffering for women, men, and all varying shades of gender.

Speaking of suffering, growing up, I was an ugly-duckling and a nerd. Actually, let me correct that – I was Conditioned to believe I was an ugly duckling and a nerd. I was constantly teased for the same things that I once hated about myself, but now through the power of self-transformation, love about myself. We each have the power to transform anything negative into something positive. Tar baby becomes beautiful dark coco skin, nappy hair becomes perfectly shaped smooth head, four eyes becomes a mystical clairvoyance through almond

30

shaped eyes, crooked overbite becomes a beautiful bright smile, Olive Oyl body become Amazonian arms and legs, my tomboyish ways are the perfect mate to my feminine nature, and flat feet are powerful roots in our Haitian culture - our Haitian Ancestors, creating the first successful slave rebellion and first Black Republic. Honor your expression or it will be lost forever and speak, knowing you are meant to survive, because we are all children of the Universe, God, Nature, Universe, Creator, Light, Energy, whatever word or non-word suits you - this one unifying energy loves us all.

I used to feel I wasn't worthy of love. Fear from my past experiences of being molested, bullied, abused in every way, homeless, suicidal, falsely and illegally arrested and imprisoned and put in a mental institution against my will – all these experiences used to keep me down. But now I rise like a phoenix from the ashes - loving myself more than I have ever loved my SELF before, through forgiveness and self-love. I forgive people, including myself, for wanting to put me in a box. Insecurity may come out in someone who feels they can't "figure you out," which, TO ME, is a reflection of their control issues that they have learned from the programming, domestication and conditioning of society through media, church, school, and some so called families and friends. But don't let that stop you, for every moment is a moment to be new so may you live your lives passionately, without compromise. Do you love yourselves out there? Well, only you can answer that. It is time to Be and Do YOU!!! So,

Peace, be still…

I am no longer defined by my mind.

Society can no longer domesticate me.

I am not conditioned by churches.

I am no longer enslaved by my family's beliefs.

The media can no longer control my decisions.

I am not my country's lies.

I am unexplainable – can you handle my mystery? Or are you too insecure?

I am unique.

I either trust and love myself – or others will enslave me.

I choose I, my Spirit.

Death does not scare me, for my Spirit is everlasting.

I am not a woman, I am not a man, I am not human, I am no-thing.

And in my no-thingness I am free.

Can you resonate with my silence?

Are you secure in my aloneness?

Don't be afraid, you are here to love.

I am no longer who I was and can no longer go back to how things were in my life.

I surrender, and burn away, my expectations, assumptions, illusions, and ambitions.

I let go of all, for all that is meant in my life appears in Divine time.

So to all I say goodbye – and thank you.

Don't be afraid to say goodbye, for that is how new beginnings arise.

I am my Beloved and am ready to receive my Beloveds.

Each and every one of you are my beloveds…we belong to each other…

I am ready to be touched, kissed, and loved – starting with My SELF.

Can our connection embrace the freeness of my fluidity?

And embrace looking into each other's eyes,

holding hands,

and embracing each other- clothed and naked?

Welcome my Nature – All of who I am – or peacefully leave me alone.

I am finally ripe and ready to fall off the tree with implicit trust…

Ready to be eaten – it is time to drink your nectar through mine.

Be in the present and be cured with me.

I pray for you all this very same Freedom – for without

Your Truth something is missing in existence.

Trust yourself, you can do it, don't give up.

Much peace and flow to you all,

Living as a meditation 24/7,

May we all cross paths in newness...

My name is MilDred

My name is DRED

I am a multi-spirited, Haitian – American, gender-illusioning, black, shaved, different, God/dess, anti-oppression, open , non-traditional, self-expressed, blessed, gender bending, drag-kinging, fluid, ancestor supported and after all that – non-labelling woMan...Womb-Man...

Now I know that's a lot but I can handle all that - after all I am a Gemini"

Www.DredLove.com

IYANIFA OYADE QUEEN HOLLINS

PUSSY POEMS OF INTENTIONAL HEALING AND RESTORATION OF POWER

THERE HAS BEEN AN ASSAULT ON PUSSIES AND WOMBS FROM THE BEGINNING OF TIME. AS WE MOVE INTO THE TWENTY-FIRST CENTURY THERE IS A CALL OR MANDATE TO ALL LIVING BEINGS, THROUGHOUT THE COSMOS AND ON PLANET EARTH, TO SHIFT THE LEGACY OF VIOLENCE AGAINST WOMEN AND GIRLS. THERE IS A CALL TO SHIFT THE ENERGETIC INHERITANCE OF MOLESTATION, RAPE AND DOMESTIC VIOLENCE. THIS CALL ALSO MANDATES THAT THE COVENANT THAT PERPETUATES THIS TYPE OF VIOLENCE CONSISTING OF SECRECY, SILENCE AND SHAME, AMONG GRANDMOTHERS AND MOTHERS, BE ERADICATED.

A POEM FOR CREATING A LEAGACY OF SAFE PUSSYS

1) I KNOW WHY THE COYOTE SCREAMS

LITTLE GIRLS, BRAIDS, BLOOD AND FUCKING DON'T GO TOGETHER

MY PUSSY SHOULD NOT BE BLEEDING YET

ITS ONLY 7 YRS NEW

THE COYOTE SCREAMS TO ALARM THAT PREMATURE BLOOD IS SPILLIN...

36

THE COYOTE SCREAMS LATE IN THE NIGHT

TO PROTECT LITTLE GIRLS WITH BRAIDS

THE COYOTE SCREAMS LATE IN THE NIGHT TO WAKE HER
MAMA

FROM THE SLUMBER OF FEAR

FROM THE SLUMBER SECRECY

FROM THE SLUMBER SHAME

THAT ALLOWD HER TO IGNORE THE SCREAMS OF THE COYOTE

WHILE

UNCIVILIZED ENTRY INTO HER DAUGHTER WAS MADE

WHILE

UNCIVILIZED ENTRY PAST HER BRAIDS

PAST HER TEDDY BEARS

PAST HER PINK BABY DOLL SHEETS

PAST THE COYOTES DAT WAS HOLLERIN

PAST

PAST

FORCFULLY PAST

BLOOD NOT YET RIPE

BLOOD THAT WOULD SOIL HER MEMORY

FOREVER

THE COYOTE SCREAMS TO STOP THE LINEAGE OF ASSUALT ON LITTLE PUSSIES

THE COYOTE SCREAMS TO CREATE A NEW LINEAGE OF FREE PUSSIES

I KNOW WHY THE COYOTE SCREAMS

HAVE YOU HEARD HER SCREAM

NEXT TIME YOU DO

WAKE UPPPPPPPPPP!!!

WE ARE THE KEEPER OF THE NEW PUSSIES

2) KEEPERS OF THE NU PUSSIES

PUSSIES FILTERING IN AND OUT, OUT AND IN THRU THE COSMOS

THERES PUSSIES EVERYWHERE,

PUSSIES IN THE TREES,

PUSSIES IN THE EARTH

PUSSIES IN THE OCEAN

PUSSIES IN THE SKY

THERE'S MIGHT EVEN BE A PUSSY READING THIS POEM

A WHOLE LOTTA PUSSIES IN THIS ROOM.....

AND THERE ARE ......

UNPROTECTED PUSSIES LANDIN IN THIS SPHERE CALLED EARTH

A RUGGED ATMOSPHERE OF UNTOLD NIGHTMARES

THEY BE CALCIFIED IN BIG MAMA TITTIES YOU KNOW

THEY SAID SHE GOT THE CANCER U KNOW BUT I KNOW ITS
THEM TALES THAT SHE AINT TELLIN US ABOUT

IT'S THOSE FEARS THAT KEEP HER BELLY SWELLIN AND SWELLIN
AND SWELLIN WIT SHAME

DOCTAS CAINT CUT IT OUT CAUSE YOU CANT CUT OUT DEM
KINDA TALES WIT A KNIFE

BEING REMOVED TO ONLY GROW BACK AGAIN...... IN SOME
UNEXPECTING NEW LITTLE PUSSY, UNDESERVING OF WHAT SHE
BOUT TA GIT

BIG MAMAS, WHOSE PUSSY NEVER GREW PAST THE AGE OF
HER TRAUMA

NOW 86 AND A PUSSY 5 AND 3 QUARTA YRS OLD YRS

STILL PLACES OF RAW INSIDE CAUSE, CAUSE DEM WOUNDS
NEVA HEALDED YOU KNOW

HER PUSSY NEVA GREW UP

HER PUSSY NEVA LAUGHED

HER PUSSY NEVA TRULY LOVE

NEVER ACCESSED HER PUSSIES STORY...YOU KNOW THE STORY
SHE BE TELLIN YOU BOUT EVERY MONTH THRU HER BLOOD,
LISTEN TO IT!

BABY PUSSIES GIVING BIRTH TO MORE BABY PUSSIES

DIDN'T KNOW HOW TO PROTECT HER BABIES PUSSY CAUSE
YOU SEE, HER PUSSY WAS STILL A BABY IT SELF

BIG MAMA KEPT UP THE LEARNED SECRECY

STAND BY YOUR PREDITOR

TURN BACK THE SHEETS

SLAPPED HER OWN CHEEK WHILE

HEARD THE SCREAMS, YEAH SHE HEARD UM

THOSE SCREAMS THAT WERE DISSOLVING HER BABIES DREAMS

SEEMS...SEEMS TO BE RIGHT YOU KNOW...DAS WHAT MY
MAMA SAY

SEEMS RIGHT YOU KNOW...I MADE IT THU

IS GON BE ALRIGHT

FOR WHO?????????????????

THE BOOK SAY STAND BY YOUR MAN

OBEY HIM TO A FAULT

TIL DEATH WE DON'T TELL

OF THE, SHHHHHHHHHHHHHHHHHHHH

THE GOOD BOOK HAS NO PSLAM TO PROTECT LITTLE PUSSIES!

NOT ONE TIME DOES THE GOOD BOOK MENTION THE WORD PUSSY!

WHY!!!!!!!!!!!!!!!!!!!!!!!!!

WRITE ONE!!!! THE PUSSIES ARE SCREAMING

WRITE US AN INVISIBLE PRAYER THAT LINES THE TENDERNESS OF OUR HYMN NU

WRITE US A PRAYER THAT PROTECTS OUR DREAMS

WRITE US A PRAYER THAT PROTECTS LITTLE GIRLS WITH BRAIDS WHILE THEY SLEEP

WRITE US A PRAYER THAT AFFIRMS WHEN TWO OR MORE PUSSIES ARE GATHERED

THEY WILL BE PROTECTED, THEY WILL BE NURTURED, THEY WILL BE LOVED

WRITE US A PRAYER!

WE ARE THE KEEPERS OF OUR SISTERS PUSSIES

WE ARE THE KEEPERS OF THE NU PUSSIES....CAN YOU GIT WIT DAT?????????????????

3) THE TEN PUSSY COMMANDMENTS

1. THOU SHALT HAVE NO FEAR WHEN PROTECTING A PUSSY.
2. THOU SHALT NOT REMAIN QUIET WHEN THERE IS THE POSSIBILITY OF DANGER TO A PUSSY. NOR SHALL ONE KNOWING PROTECT A SUSPECTED PUSSY PREDITOR
3. THOU SHALT NOT TAKE THE NAME OF THE PUSSY IN VAIN.

4. REMEMBER THE PUSSY AND KEEP HER HOLY.

5. HONOR THY PUSSY, HER BLOOD AND THY MOTHER EARTH.

6. THOU SHALT NOT TOUCH A PUSSY BEFORE HER TIME, WITH COHERSION OR WITHOUT MUTUAL CONSENT WITH AN ADULT PUSSY.

7. THOU SHALT NOT COMMIT RAPE OR MOLESTATION OR ANY VIOLATION TO A PUSSY OF ANYKIND.

8. THOU SHALT NOT STEAL PUSSY

9. THOU SHALT NOT BEAR FALSE WITNESS WHEN YOU HEAR A PUSSY SCREAM OR AGAINST AN ACCUSED PUSSY PREDITOR.

10. THOU SHALT NOT COVET A PUSSY, UNLESS IT IS YOUR OWN.

4) MY PUSSY AMERICA

MY PUSSY, 'TIS OF THEE,
SWEET LAND FOR ALL TO BE

OF THEE I SCREAM;
LAND THAT MY FATHERS TORE

LAND THAT MY MOTHERS IGNORED
A QUEEN MISTAKEN FOR A WHORE

LET ALL PUSSIES FREE

5) THEY SAY MY PUSSY SMELLS STRANGE

SMELLS LIKE BLACK SOULS LINGERING ON THE OCEAN'S FLOOR

SMELLS LIKE MY DADDY'S DRINKING BUDDY NEXT DOOR

SMELLS LIKE THE SUNDAY SCHOOL TEACHERS RAPE

SMELLS LIKE THE PUBERTY BLOOD I FORSAKED

SMELLS LIKE ASTROIDS THEY CALL FIBRIODS THAT SUCK UP MY CBC'S

SMELLS LIKE I DON'T KNOW WHO THE PINT OF BLOOD
CAME FROM I RECEIVED

SMELLS LIKE THE IRISH BLOOD I IGNORE

SMELLS LIKE MY DEPRESSION TELLING ME I DON'T
WANNA BE HERE NO MORE

IT SMELLS LOOSE, IT SMELLS TIGHT

IT SMELLS LIKE A TOXIC WASTE SITE

SMELLS LIKE THE IRAQ WAR AND THE WARS BEFORE AND
BRFORE

OH NO I THINK SOMETHING JUST TORE

SMELLS LIKE MARIJUANA, LIKE WEED

IT SMELLS LIKE MY ABORTED UNBORN SEED

SMELLS LIKE CAMBODIAN CHILD PROSTITUTION

DAMN, CAN MY WOMB GET SOME RESTITUTION!

SMELLS LIKE CONGOLESE BABIES WITH AIDS

SMELLS LIKE DOPE HOUSE RAIDS

SMELLS LIKE PIG EARS, MY MOTHERS FEARS

SMELLS LIKE DOMESTIC VIOLENCE, SELF-HATRED AND
TEARS

SMELLS LIKE SCREAMS IN THE NIGHT

SMELLS LIKE I GOTTA KEEP UP THIS FIGHT

SMELLS LIKE THE CAT MY UNCLE MADE ME KICK

SMELLS LIKE HIS PRIVATE I DIDN'T WANNA LICK

SMELLS LIKE INTERNALIZED OPPRESSION

SMELLS LIKE A CATHOLIC CONFESSION

SMELLS LIKE THE LIES OF THE CHURCH

SMELLS LIKE THE PASTOR LIPS PERCHED

SMELLS LIKE A STILL BORN DEATH

SMELLS LIKE THE CHOIR BOYS BED THE PRIEST JUST LEFT

SMELLS LIKE PHARMACEUTICLS, ANTIBIOTICS AND DIFLUCCAN

OH MY GOODNESS I THINK MY PUSSY IS PUKIN

SMELLS LIKE THE LIES IN ALL THE SCHOOL BOOKS I READ

IT SMELLS LIKE THE ULTRASHEEN PERM STILL IN MY HEAD

SMELLS LIKE THE GOOD BACTERIA SAYING THEY ATE UP ALL OF US

IT SMELLS LIKE I NEED SOME ACIDOCPHILIS

IT SMELLS LIKE GMO'S

IT SMELLS LIKE CRACK HOES

SMELLS LIKE RED, YELLOW, BROWN, BLACK AND WHITE FACES

IT SMELLS LIKE THE PAIN OF ALL THE RACES

IT SMELLS LIKE I HATE YOU

IT SMELLS LIKE YOU HATE ME TOO

BUT WE DON'T WANT TO

IT SMELLS LIKE DEATH

IT SMELLS LIKE LIFE

IT SMELLS LIKE ME

IT SMELLS LIKE YOU

IT SMELLS LIKE WE GOTTA LOTTA WORK LEFT TO DO

IT SMELLS LIKE A PHOENIX RISING INTO LIBERATION

IT SMELLS LIKE ITS OVER DUE FOR A CELEBRATION

A REDEDICATION TO LIFE

TO THRIVE

TO REMEMEBR HER FRAGRANCE INSIDE

IT SMELLS LIKE SHE WANTS TO BIRTH A NEW
CIVILIZATION, A WHOLISTIC NATION

IT SMELLS LIKE ME

IT SMELLS LIKE YOU

IT SMELLS LIKE WE GOTTA LOTTA WORK LEFT TO DO

ASE.

CHANNELLED AND WRITTEN BY QUEEN L. HOLLINS

BRIDGET (BEY) CELESTE

Short Story-Parental Discretion by Bridget (Bey) Celeste

I never told Mama I was gay. I never told Daddy either, but I felt
he knew. He asked Sister "Is she *funny*?" When Sister told me
what he had asked, I felt sick. I remember it well. I locked
myself in her bathroom, turned the water on and cried into to her
peach hand towels. I felt scared and ashamed of my parents
knowing about my attraction to women. They raised me with a
strong belief in God and I did not want to be a young un-Godly
woman with homosexual tendencies. I was afraid of going to hell
and I did not want to embarrass my parents.

I got pregnant when I was twenty-two. I never had a problem
catching men. I am a big girl with a pretty face. I have been told
that for as long as I can remember but I never really knew if it
meant I was actually pretty. I guess it did not matter much at that
time because the boys on East 8th Street thought I was pretty
enough. That is where I met him, a quiet soft spoken guy with
dark, deep set eyes. He had dimples like mine and his mustache
made him look older than his actual age. He was comfortable
and felt safe. He was perfect for what I needed, which was a
cover to deflect suspicions.

We were a couple, off and on, for a few years. I did not care
about his indiscretions with other women during our time
together. I just needed his protection against the questions at
family gatherings when everyone began asking why I wasn't
married yet. They questioned me about my tomboyish attire.
They started asking me about a schoolmate I spent time with
also. "She is a close friend", I would reply and she was. I could
not tell anyone I was in love with her, not even her. There was
no need to. I had a man, a baby on the way and that was the way
I thought it was supposed to be.

When the baby was born I could see the relief in Daddy's eyes.
Mama was happy but, I was far from contentment. I let the
boyfriend slip away and vowed celibacy. That is what a young
Godly woman should do after bearing a child out of wedlock. As
hard as it was to hear the judgmental comments, I welcomed

them with open arms. They were far better than what I would face if everyone knew my true desire. Yet I prayed those desires away every Sunday at the altar. I bore my singleness and celibacy with determination, but I never thought it would be six years before I was kissed again.

The first time I heard her voice I believed I was listening to pure sex. I had never been struck by a voice before, but hers touched me in ways I only fantasized about in the dark. She was feminine and strong. A perfect concoction that rendered me drunk and sober at the same time. I wanted her but she would not allow it. She said I was too afraid and controlled by the belief of others. She told me I had to find my peace and that she could not stand in the closet with me. I had some decisions to make. I was unwilling to live another six years unhappy and alone.

I met her by accident. She interchanged the last two numbers and kept leaving messages about switching shifts at work on my phone. When we finally spoke to straighten out the mix-up, I could not say goodbye when the time came. I blurted out, "Would you like to have lunch?" She said, "Sure." A week later she kissed me, and before the kiss ended I knew I wanted a woman kissing me for the rest of my life.

In my secret world I loved women, but openly they were co-workers and old acquaintances. I was only fooling myself, however. My family and friends questioned everything I did and who I was doing it with. Mama was concerned, but quiet. Sister was clearly upset. So upset she outed me, to Daddy and our Pastor. "She dealing in homosexuality…" is what they told me she said.

When Pastor called me I felt that initial shame all over again. Shortly afterwards I was alienated and felt intensely ostracized. I lost many I called friend and I lost Sister for more than a year. She came around, as well as a few others, but it was never the same.   Mama and Daddy, they were my saving grace.

I was terrified of what my parents would have to say. My mind conjured every possible rejection. I hid myself away from them, awaiting angry phone calls and unannounced visits, but for more than a year nothing happened. The long silence was worse than my fears. I took a stance and decided to go to them.

I was prepared for rejection from my parents. I never believed they would accept me as their lesbian daughter. I had cowered in the thought for so long that I could not imagine anything else coming from them. But the beautiful gift about parents who love their children is they love their children unconditionally. Surprisingly, Daddy told me I owed him no explanations. I came from his flesh and there could be nothing wrong with the way I was. Mama said, "You being gay don't mean nothing to me. I know who you are. You are my daughter and a child of God. That's the only thing that will ever matter."

With my parents embrace, years of distrust and doubt dissolved away. They had finally given me the liberty and pride I had silently longed for. I was now able to be myself fully and without apology. Being me was something I never believed I would ever have to the courage to do, but my parents help made it a reality.

SPHEAR

COLLINS

Poetic Reflections on Coming Out

How do I tell my Mom and Dad that I'm a fag?
Give me a plastic bag, so I can throw up.
Put it over my head, tie it tight, until I blow up.
That's how I felt since I was four.
We were poor and I wanted more.
Every night I prayed that Snow White would walk
through my door.
When the whole family went to Disneyland, I stood in
line anxiously to kiss Snow White.
My Auntie changed my plans.
She told me that girls can only kiss a man.
I didn't understand.
I started to cry, scream and demand.
Finally she said, "kiss her, if you want to then, FREAK."
And I did.
I wish I could remember the exact day of the week.
I felt so weak.
I should still seek some sort of counseling, but my brain
keeps cancelling.
I've had accidents and can't even remember.
My foggiest days are in December.
Maybe it's the presents.
So, from this point and that point, I've needed a joint, to
deal with the blows to the joints.
I mean, here I am different and indifferent and I'm
someone who could've been, wanted to be so perfect.
I was so hopeful.
It was awful growing up with this secret: I'm humping
girls and loving it!!
Then, I started breaking off baby dolls arms, burying
earrings, barretes, charms.
Obviously setting off parental alarms.

Oh no, here comes the rebelliousness. I'm not going to wear that dress!!

Oh yes, it's been a mess. From Juvenile hall to County, trying to find me.

Why else would I be in her? Without her fur, I'd surely wither.

I would be so bitter, like a desperate house wife. Hell no. I choose life. The God in me is bigger than my enemy and told me to simply be free."Love first and be blessed. Love yourself for you are a test.... to see if those who believe in me, prove it, by loving you unconditionally. I want you to do you."

 And so it is. And so it shall be. Thank you God, for loving me.

Poem-Duplicate

I need to duplicate myself, so that more of me can be inside of you. I don't think you have any idea how deep inside of me you really are. I've allowed you to penetrate areas unknown to man.....I'm afraid. My vulnerability inhibits me. I am so afraid, that's why occasionally I go on little hissy fits. Or is it that the makeup sex is like physics? Who can explain that shit? Mouth to mouth, clit to clit, perfectly positioned for orgasmic....mmm, mmm, mmm, it's one of my favorites. Do you know why? Because, I get to hold the back of your neck with my teeth, like the lions do. Get all up in your ear, my middle finger all in your rear. Baby, your insides....they pour these peaches and i just hold my mouth there. I'm so thirsty. Hoping to get a lifetime supply of your fruit juices. It's worth drowning for. Your soul bears the burdens of the world and so does mine. We share the same sign, now slow wine for me. Let me smack that ass a few times. Tell me it's mine. I wish I were a rat. I'd run inside of you, straight to your heart. I want to fuck you in the grocery store in a shopping cart. We're up to three fingers now. When are you going to get serious and let me live in you? If you relax, get your mind right, i could put a chair in there. Oatmeal honey crusted nipples, you've got my stomach doing ripples. I need to duplicate myself, maybe even triples. To get to your subtle sultry, yet always ready with rebuttals. Since we can't make babies, let's keep making these puddles.....I love sucking your toes. With or without the stilettos.

muviesmoveme@yahoo.com

KATHY
FULLER

Essay-Honeymoon

The time was April of 1999, a few months after the state of Hawaii passed a law making gay marriage in Hawaii illegal.* Gay couples were still getting married, albeit, not legally, but I still called it marriage, and chose to have a wedding. Tammi and I had planned on a Hawaiian vacation anyway, so after she agreed to marry me, we decided to get married in Hawaii. It was all planned quickly, so we went alone, without family or friends.

A little about Tammi: She is the only person I ever asked to marry me and I would marry her again in a heartbeat. I knew within a short time of meeting her, that I wanted her in my life forever. She had a warmth, a beauty, a tenderness, a strength, and so many other fine attributes, that I was happy just to know her as a person. She was a gorgeous and outgoing typical Leo - one who liked being in the spotlight and the center of attention. The total opposite of me. We complemented each other. She was the yin to my yang, and vice versa. I loved her so much I told everyone I was getting married, including having an engagement party at work and a family party where everyone was invited.

We chose the beautiful isle of Maui, to get married in a tropical paradise. I had been a member of the predominately gay denomination Metropolitan Community Church, or MCC for short, in the past. It had branches across the country, including one on Oahu, in Honolulu, Hawaii. There was no MCC on Maui, at that time, so we arranged for the pastor of MCC Honolulu, Reverend Bill, to come to Maui to officiate our wedding.

Reverend Bill was a tall, thin man with white hair and a cheery but wise disposition. He reminded me of Mister Rogers, from the old television show for children. He was a state licensed minister and although gay marriage was not legal, the ceremony was performed just as though it had been. We each had a counseling session with him and signed church documents and registries. He brought 2 member of his church with him to witness the wedding. It turns out, that my wife knew one of the witnesses, who was an activist from Sacramento. They had known each other through work in the gay and lesbian community in Sacramento, where my wife lived. Her name was Annie Runningfeather, a short, talkative woman with auburn hair, and lots of energy. The other witness was a younger white woman named Sarah, who also acted as the photographer.

Tammi and I did not have a location picked out for our wedding, but she wanted it to be held outside in nature. We listened to a few suggestions and decided on a mountain area looking over the island. We drove up there with the Reverend and Annie and Sarah. The place was crowded with cars and tourists, so we decided to go look for a private spot on the beach to do the ceremony. We drove up the coast and finally settled on a secluded sport with a small grove of narrow trees, right on the beach. There were a few surfers and sunbathers further down the beach, but no one close to us.

Encircled by a cluster of trees, Tammi and I changed into the white gauze-type outfits that she had picked out for our wedding. We had blouses with long sleeves and matching pants, similar to East Indian style clothing. Her neckline and cuffs were trimmed in gold ribbon. My outfit was plain. Sarah presented us each a traditional Hawaiin wedding lei, covered with white ti plants. Reverend Bill wore a white short-sleeved shirt and a clerical collar.

In my head, I was nervous and just wanted to get the ceremony over with. I was harboring fear and concern that we would be verbally or physically attacked by some mob of homophobes. No one else seemed to share my concern. Reverend went to getting his notes together. Tammi was getting her outfit together. Annie picked up on my concern and said the island was friendly with the "hang-loose" atmosphere and that no one would bother us. We moved from the tiny grove of thin trees to closer to the waves to begin the wedding.

Tammi and I wrote our own vows, which we said to one another after the Reverend said his obligatory remarks. We looked into each other's eyes and I tried not to cry. I made my promises and intentions known to the woman I loved so deeply. I produced some gold wedding bands, as a surprise to Tammi. (She had brought some garish silver rings back in Los Angeles, but they had been returned to the store, at my request). After our vows, we kissed on the beach and Annie Littlefeather snapped still photos. To my amazement and horror, I heard the sound of clapping. Unbeknownst to me, during our ceremony, the beachgoers came and watched from a respectful distance of around 20 feet. At the appropriate moment, they gave us a rousing round of applause. My fears were unfounded that day on the beach. No one said anything negative and we were not attacked in any way.

Later that evening, we went to a casual-dress Italian restaurant with Rev Bill for a wedding dinner. There was coincidentally a waitress there who looked and spoke just like my wife's late mother. It was very emotional for her to see someone who reminded her so much of her Mom. The waitress was very friendly and talked to us about places to visit on Maui, and how she had visited California before. I felt very comfortable with her, so I couldn't help but tell her that we had just gotten married. The other waiters and cook came over and gave us congratulations. Tammi was astonished that I had actually come out to these total strangers, but I was so happy. I was full of love, and had forgotten to be fearful. I wanted everyone to feel the love I was feeling.

That was one of the happiest times in my life.

The next day my new wife and I went on a sightseeing tour by van. There were about 9 people all together in the van. Tammi and I were the only black people on the tour. There was a young couple, who were on their honeymoon. The tour guide gave them special mention. Tammi said to me that she wished we could tell everyone that it was our honeymoon too. She wanted to be acknowledged as a newlywed, but I didn't think it was a good idea to state our gayness to a van full of straight strangers, so we did not. We sat through the tour letting them think we were friends on a vacation. I felt bad for not having the courage to tell the truth.

My marriage to Tammi did not last, but I will always cherish her and remember the time we had together on Maui. I wish I didn't have to deal with fear of reprisal for being gay, because there are so many other challenges that come up in relationships. My fear has subsided over the years, with the progress made in gay visibility, but it has not disappeared completely.

- Note: Names in this story have been changed to respect the privacy of the individuals.

- *Following a 1993 decision by the Hawaii State Supreme Court that found the state's refusal to grant same-sex couples marriage licenses discriminatory, voters in 1998 approved a constitutional amendment granting the Hawaii State Legislature the power to reserve marriage to opposite-sex couples, which resulted in a law banning same-sex marriage.
- On February 16, 2011, Hawaii's House passed the civil unions bill that will allowing same-sex and different-sex couples to enter into a civil union. Governor Neil Abercrombie signed the bill on February 24, 2011 and civil unions will begin on January 1, 2012.

CANDACE
EBONE'
MEALY

Poem-Your Silence Will Not Protect You (Audre Lorde)- By
Candace Ebone' Mealy

It protects liberating truths
creating the entombment of victims
who shed tears of blood
scratching at the walls
of their mothers wombs
fearing
being hellbound
on a planet
that was meant for bliss
but instead has been
handed over to demons

It rapes
men, women, and children
of their righteousness

Honesty no longer
gets a pat on the pack
or gives kudos
now
it throws you
under the bus
the first chance it gets

Tire burns
are the churns
of word war fare
from
the toungues
of liars revealed

Their achilles heel
of survival revealed

scribed in unearthed diaries
and court documents
of their victims
in which time
hasn't been kind
to them

Their weathered skin
thinning hair
and heavy eyelids
with damn near
blind iris'
which have
traumatization
etched in them
like a suicide concoction
have just enough
vision left in them
to aim
a finger of blame
before
silence completely
kills them
because
there weren't
enough trees
on land
to create
enough papyrus
to turn up the volume
of written pain

Silence was the gas mileage
of insomnia and insanity
from the point
of victimization
and it created
the temptation and addiction
that I have
for lead and ink
The courage to form
every written word
came from the desire
to live stress free
even if
for just a second
longer.......

Essay-"There is a light that shines special for you and me" ~Common: The Light

We so often believe that we will find you in religious rhetoric & our dogmatic beliefs make us think that you exist in temples of mass spiritual destruction, but I have found you in the depths of my solitude and I have rejoiced in our presence. Just me and you - and the truth.

Qurans & Bibles could not speak to me the way you have reached out and touched me in the breath of natures bosom, offering me life when those around could only offer survival.

You have showed yourself in the smiles of strangers and the laughter of children and it makes me wonder how anyone could misconstrue your existence. Yes, you have created beauty but in our self destructive nature which is at the core of humanity we have created the ugly that we believe is of your doing.

You have given us this planet in all of its diversity to embrace yet we reject it for its unknown properties fearing what we'll find if we bask in it with complete blind faith. We are not true believers but boast misinterpreted scriptures as we burn in man-made hell fires of self damnation.

Thank you for our private sojourns in which you have revealed your essence unto me. I enjoy singing to you, singing for you, dancing with you, dancing for you, laughing because of you, laughing with you, conversations, conversations and more conversations between us.

I know you're right. No one would believe me if I told them so I'll just enjoy the fact that I know that while they ridicule themselves and degrade one another, that you are watching and waiting until they make the same realization and they relax into it.

I won't tell our secret but I admit that it's hard to sit back and watch our communities blunder and dim their own lights and lose their way possibly never to return but I have faith that you'll guide the deserving back on to the right path where I will be waiting for them with you......All Of My Love,Your Angel Sunday: April 21, 2002

Poem-Untitled

Once upon a time…….

I used to be
ambidextrious
til a
stroke
left me
damn near
motionless.

It would be my equilibrium,
speech,
and left side
completely affected…

….2 days later
when
I got up
and walked
the lament changed
from the
youngest stroke patient
to
you're not supposed
to be doing that yet
and
when I overcame
most of my
impediments
folks talked about
how blessed
I am.

What no one
really understands

is
that I refused
to exit
stage left
even
at the most
depressing moment
when
I thought
I was moving
my whole body
only
to look over
and realize
I WASN'T
I remained motivated
to take
my next breath.

Survivor of
molestation, incest,
and rape
-witness to
domestic violence

I remain
unconvinced
that THIS is
my time of death.

The baggage
I discard
so life
can begin

I've got battle scars
gushing

more blood
than your
heart

May be wounded
but
I aint quit
the fight
yet

I let my lyrics
hit you
with
the final blow
 to your chest

winded
by my verbs
because you
underestimated
my will

If lyrics could kill
where you stand
would be your
funeral!

So,
when you
size up
this female
you might need
correctional lenses
for your pupils
cuz
everything you see
aint even

half of me....

...assume nothing
I may be
the runt of the litter
but
I've seen
more dark days
than the moon
and I still beam
like the sun
as I stand
before you!

DALE

GUY

MADISON

ESSAY-I'M COMING OUT

My first gay crush was on my best friend in high school.
I lived in a small navy town in Portsmouth Virginia. His
name was Bruce Melvin. We both were in the drama
department. Bruce was cool, light-skinned and had a
huge perfect smile set in a handsome, square jaw. He
had the deepest voice I ever heard for a guy at sixteen.
We both wore our hair in the huge Afros of the day, his
in a square shape to match his face and mine in a fitting
oval. He was ultra smooth with girls and had scored
many sexual conquests. Whereas I had only been with
three girls before I met my girlfriend, Bruce had been
with dozens. Once, when we were engaged in a
conversation with some female friends, Bruce made an
argument in favor of oral sex; he reasoned that it was
cleaner than kissing because fewer germs reached the
vagina than the average mouth. It made sense to me at
the time -- until I realized that it takes a mouth to
perform oral sex!

Being around Bruce was fun. We had been best friends
since fourth grade, even after he took the lead away
from me in the play *No Man Is An Island*. He had
played Marley's ghost to my Scrooge in *A Christmas
Carol* the year that my voice changed and I almost lost
the role of Ebenezer Scrooge. He gave me the nickname
I had always wanted, calling me "Big D," D as in
"Dale," not "dick." I was taller than him by half an
inch. He was a little guy. I called him Lil' Stud
because he was such a ladies' man. One night after play
rehearsal, we got high and I confessed my feelings for
him. He rejected me but promised to remain my friend.
We made an oath to meet up at NYU and become

famous actors. It was hard looking in his face after that incident.

I devised a plan that would change the course of my life. My parents were divorced and my father lived in Baltimore. When my father came to visit, I told him that a man had molested me in a Norfolk peep store and I had started smoking weed as a result. To sweeten the story, I told him that I had hidden a bag in the house. I told him I was afraid to be in Portsmouth because I thought the man would try to come back and do something to me. My father took me out of school the next day and I packed my bags to go live with him in Baltimore. After arriving to Baltimore, I realized I had made a huge mistake. I was entering my senior year with all new friends. I missed Bruce terribly. Although living in Baltimore city allowed me more of an opportunity to meet other gay people, I was still very confused inside.

It was 1976, my senior year at Baltimore's Northwestern High School that my sexuality really blossomed. I lucked up in drama department when I entered the class of Michael DeBoy. This was long before money cuts from arts programs. The school produced several productions a year. My first production at my new school was the play *Day of Absence*. We were entered in a regional one-act play festival. The night before the festival, I tried to commit suicide. To this day, I cannot explain why I was so depressed that I took a handful of aspirin and drank cough syrup. I believe I blocked out the memories of the fear and confusion I was going through at the time. I left home and sat underneath an expressway hoping never to wake up. I feel asleep and the cold night air woke me up as I vomited. I walked home with a huge headache thinking that was a bad idea.

Ironically, the role I played in *Day of Absence* was a husband whose wife wakes him out of a deep sleep to tell him that the "mammy" is missing. The dark comedy is a story of what happens to a city of townsfolk who wake up one day to find all the "black" people missing. I will never forget one of the comments given to me that day was how believable my performance was as the sleep husband.

My next production was the musical *Godspell*. The experience evoked memories of my sixth grade production of *A Christmas Carol*. I had to learn the song "We Beseech Thee" for the role of Jeffrey and, while I was a great actor and dancer, my singing was not supreme. Mr. DeBoy replaced me halfway through the production but later called me back, just as Mr. Brown had done in the sixth grade for my role as Scrooge in *A Christmas Carol*; He told me he would rather have an actor who couldn't sing than a singer who couldn't act. He made me join the gospel choir and take voice lessons to up my game.

Though my singing was off tempo, at least my voice did not crack! Making it through that production is what allowed me to get closer to Eddie Greene, my second crush.

Eddie was chubby and light-skinned with big, full, beautiful lips. He had long eyelashes and wavy hair, cut in a "shag" style. The Afro was beginning to play out, and the shag haircut was what guys were transitioning into. The best way to describe it is that it was the black version of the mullet haircut. Eddie was playing the lead of Jesus in the production of *Godspell*. Every time we would rehearse his death scene on the cross, you would have thought the real Jesus Christ had died up in that theater. He was loud but talented. In fact, he was voted "Most Talented," out of the senior class. We started going out and began a torrid affair.

Being a boyfriend to the most popular kid in school made me feel special. Our affair was very passionate. Eddie and I would cut class and make love in his car, or slip away to the park or spend the afternoon in his home when his mother was at work. In those days, kids who were having sex would wear their hickeys on their necks, (or wherever else on their body!), as a medal of honor. It was an advertisement that told all your friends, "Hey, look at me -- I'm having sex." It was like all those broken blood vessels were actually something to be proud of or a source of pride.

One day I came home and my dad asked, "Which girlfriend put that hickey on your neck?"

I proudly responded, "Or boyfriend?"

My arrogance surprises me to this very day. Foolish high school love makes a person feel like Superman. I felt like nothing could hurt me because I had the love of Eddie Greene.

My father walked out of the house. When he returned twenty minutes later, he told me that I had to move out of his home. My life changed in that moment. I knew I did not want to move back to Portsmouth, Virginia. I had four more months of high school.

My dreams of going to NYU to study acting had just flown out the window. With my father disowning me, I wouldn't be able to get his financial information to provide to NYU in consideration for financial assistance. In addition, I had to figure out where I was going to live. While my friends would be preparing for the high school prom, I would be shopping for an apartment and just trying to graduate.

Fate must have known that NYU was just a dream, because Bruce ended up going to Syracuse University that fall. The week before he was to leave for college, he came to visit me at my little ghetto apartment. We shared my fold-out sofa bed, never touching, but I craved his body. We hung out every day and went to see movies. We saw the film *Cooley High*, the African-American version of *American Graffiti,* complete with Motown music. I imagined that it was our story up on the screen. Bruce was ladies' man Richard "Cochise" Morris and I was nerdy Leroy "Preach" Jackson, who left town to become a writer.

Because I worked the night shift, our time during the day was limited because I had to sleep part of the day away. As the week drew near its end, I played hooky just to hang out with him on his last night. I told him again how much I wanted him. He told me again that he could not and would not be with me in that way. In a final act of desperation, I swallowed a whole bottle of aspirin and refused to speak to him. Bruce called an ambulance. The medics told him that I wouldn't die from an overdose of aspirin, but that I'd be very nauseous. They kept me a few days for observation at the hospital. When I returned home, Bruce had left for college. I would not see him for many years after that.

My first year of "out" gay life held its share of dark moments. I had attempted suicide twice. I was young, inexperienced and did not have a mentor to talk to

76

about what was happening to me. There were no gay talk groups or community centers to go to where I could find other young gay people out on their own. I had made an enormous step out into an unfamiliar world and I wasn't quite sure what to do next. I was living on instinct, determined never to live life in a closet. Even today, my friends know that I leave all closet doors open in my house. It became my personal mission to teach all straight people that gay people are basically no different from them. We do not have three heads. Most of us are not even recognizable. What is there to be afraid of? We just have sex with the same sex instead of the opposite sex. Everything else is pretty much the same. I don't dislike heterosexuals just because they have heterosexual sex.

A buddy of mine, not knowing I was gay, once went on incessantly about a hot lap dance he'd received from a busty female at a strip club. Instead of pretending that women were my sexual interest, I shared with him an experience I'd had with a male stripper at a gay bar. After he picked his face up off the floor, he had to admit that he respected me for being open and for treating my gay life just as normally as he treated his straight life. Yeah, that's me, spreading universal acceptance by <u>teaching one straight person at a time.</u>

The year 1976 represents more for me than just the bicentennial of the Declaration of Independence or the year I turned eighteen, the year I took my first legal drink, voted, or moved out on my own. It was the year I stumbled out of the closet and fell on my face, got up, knocked the dirt off and said, "Hey, look at me. I am gay and it does get better."

Shaashawn S.
Dial

ASSEMBLY

"I love dykes in white pants," she said to me.
I laughed.
Nodding my head in agreement as the cool Baltimore air hit
us.
My pause was incomplete before I began my confessions.

I too am in love with dykes in flowing nylon pants,
cuffed pants,
shined leather loafers,
ribbed t-shirts underneath silk screened button up shirts,
pantsuits,
tailored slacks.

I too am in love with my black lesbians of favorite hues,
deep brown soil,
red clay brown,
new roasted brown.

In a weekend I've been moved,
to move to a new city and concentrate my efforts on being
eternally single.
Enjoying the abundance of God's blessing – black women.
Eternity will come to an end before I could taste and lay
claim to all my tomboy girls,
soft butches,
girl boys,
experienced older butches,
locked sisters with cowrie shells on the tip of their jet black
or auburn truth,
natural women in short and high crowns of picked 'fros,
cut low smoothed fades,
to micro braids.

And despite all of my images,
that are comforting and home to me,
I hear the sarcasm and disgust in my father's voice
saying...
"Everything that feels good,
 isn't good for you."
And...
"Everyone who smiles in your face doesn't have your best
interest at heart."

My belly fills with the salt water my eyes restrain,
daily I live with the knowledge that my bed sheet decisions
affect him,
and the dreams for a normal life he believes it is my
responsibility to give him.
 I try to put a heterosexual label on my heart,
despite the fact that it wants no part of any category.
But to be a sensual heart.
Able to love both,
destined to choose one over the other.
Eventually making a choice,
sacrificing a part of myself.

RULES FOR "THE LIFE"

Don't drastically change your style or they'll know.
Introduce rainbow into your clothes - slowly.
Slip the pronouns to "he".
Vagueness is the key.
Use they, one, we.

Oh, here come the jokes and the stereotypes.
Thank God your name is unisex,
you could go either way.
 Hey isn't that a funny double pun to say.

My little secret always on my mind.
I think your name has changed to,
my best friend,
my good friend,
my sister without blood,
my soror,
all of the above.

I couldn't say "she", oh what blasphemy.
If you do, pick what you are,
there are only 2 classes you could be,
butch or femme no in-between.
Hurry up and classify yourself too,
lesbian, straight or bi-.
Just who are you?

No in-between-ness,
'cause you'll cause a problem.
Get "in the life" or stay out,
or you're part of the problem.
You'll be accused of just dippin',
following up on curiosity.
Not meeting a genetic need.

You can't just come to get the cookie,
without paying a price.
You'll leave a bad impression.
A horrible taste in their mouth.

A new ideology.
A new view on life.
A second culture to which I enter,
in search of my womanhood.

E
3-day-old fuzzy cornrows
6'1
Egyptian eyes
Skin the color of baking chocolate
222 lbs
full lips
tongue's flashback to salt kissed skin
thick eyebrows

dripping sweat
thick trembling thighs
watching eyes
full behinds
verbal admissions of drawn body conclusions

quieted insecurities in loud profound silence
water breaks
long brown arms wrap like ribbon
tattoos illuminated via hand held scented candles
exaggerated hip walks to bathrooms for pee breaks
relaxed exhausted muscles
foreplay for hours
deep post pleasure sleep in an ebony chest
momma's boy
incredible chemistry

DRIVE BY x 3

MARCH DRIVE BY
He possess hands big enough to hold my history and veins thick enough to hold the oneness of our mixing bloods that is the future.

JUNE DRIVE BY
He caught my nose before he caught my eye. I knew you were a well-groomed man because your dollars even smelled good.

NOVEMBER DRIVE BY

You fall like water at my feet that nourish me,
helping vines to grow,
up my spine,
making me a live flower.

If
If I stand before you in ebony naturalness,
covered only with an anklet, hand jewelry, and a grin.
Will you stand before me in ebony naturalness,
covered only from ankle to toe in Timbs and a grin?

Shaashawn
Editor-In-Chief
STUDS MAGAZINE...
Celebrating the HANDSOMELY BEAUTIFUL WOMEN
P.O. Box 3794, Harrisburg, PA 17105
www.studsmagazine.com
www.myspace.com/studsmagazine
www.downelink.com/studsmagazine
www.twitter.com/studsmagazine

ENNIS
JACKSON

Essay-FINDING ME
My Journey and the Struggles I Have Endured Because of My Identity

As a child, I was called gay, faggot, sissy and punk. My father called me those things long before I ever knew what they meant. Over time, it was clear that those words were synonymous with: disapproval, shame, sin, not allowed, nasty and unacceptable. I didn't want to be any of those things and as I became more aware of the potential for each word to be lived out in me; I spent a lot of time and energy trying to ensure that they didn't. And, while I was busy trying *not* to "be", I denied myself the opportunity to "be;" to understand how to live and to truly examine what those words meant to my life.

There was the issue of shame. I tried not to bring public shame to my family or to myself. In my mind, the public viewed me as the epitome of shame. If they perceived something as being unacceptable or wrong and I did those things, I would be the cause of shame. It was hard because it seemed to me that the 'shame list' touched nearly every area of my life.

To merely be myself was to bring shame. I couldn't tell people who I was, because it was shameful to be gay! For people to know would be the worst kind of shame. So, I was taught, "Whatever you do, keep it to yourself. Everybody don't need to know your business."

It was bad enough to be gay, but to let people know was unacceptable. So, I learned how to keep secrets; how to not be myself; how to hold things in.

I couldn't go anywhere publicly where 'they' might be. So I learned all the dark, out of the way places. I found pleasure in things and places that I should have never been exposed to. I established friendships with people that 'they' didn't know. I created unhealthy interactions because I couldn't bring my *whole* self into any setting. I learned behaviors that were unsafe and unhealthy for me because that was the norm in those places. I learned how to disguise myself and hide.

In my home, I had to behave and dress a certain way. No cursing. No smoking. No talking back. No getting out of line. No dancing. No worldly music. No bad company. Stand up straight. Speak up. Be neat. Be clean. Dress nice.

I learned that what people could see meant more than what they couldn't. So, I learned eye service and proper protocol.

More than anything though, was the issue of sin. I didn't want to be a sinner. That would keep me from going to heaven, stop God's blessings, and cause God's wrath to come. Sin separated me from God. So I learned how to lie. I learned how to put on masks. I learn how to be fake. I learned how to be deceitful.

Wanting approval and acceptance so desperately, I thought that presenting myself in ways pleasing to each group was my only hope. So, I hid the real me. I didn't want people to see me as sinful, shameful, nasty, or wrong. Yet, I wanted so desperately for everyone to approve it. Because approving *it* would mean approval of *me*. But, how could anyone else approve something I disapproved of myself? How could anyone accept me when I never exposed the *real* me?

I often wondered if they could see it; my insecurities, overcompensation, my fear. I wondered if they could see through the masks. The masks I wore to work, to church, to kick it with the boys. I always wondered and before I knew it someone would ask, "Is he gay?" Someone else would say, "You know he's a punk. " This hurt because I worked so hard to hide it. So, how could they see it? Why would they say that?

Looking back, I know that they could see it because it was the truth, regardless of my actions. It showed up in me because it was me. I believe, that my father called me those horrible names because he saw *me*. My mother kept me close and stopped me from boxing like my father and older brother because she saw *me*. My sisters taught me to stand up for myself, to do for myself. My brother rarely wanted me around. Why? They saw me too. The whole time they saw the *real* me.

As an adult, I began releasing my fear of those awful words and their definitions. But issues of shame and acceptance continued to bind me. Over time, I came to accept what they meant to me. I started seeing myself differently. I started to accept the truth and denounce the lies.

The truth is that I *am* gay. I *am* a same gender loving person. I *am* a man who values romantic interactions with persons of my own gender. But, I am *not* a faggot- a rude, disrespectful, classless, over the top man. And I'm certainly nobody's punk.

And now, I know that, there is no shame in that.

There is no shame in being who God created me to be. People's thoughts and feelings are no longer my concern. Their beliefs no longer affect me. What they think, feel and/ or believe does not effect me. I am no longer fearful. I am no longer shameful. I am no longer unacceptable. Truthfully, I never was. I am Strong. I am Black. I am a Man. I am Gay. I am ME!

DAVID PAYNE

Poem-SHIP DISAPPEAR

My ship had gone
Sailed away
Now the waves are coming back
Holding their place
Strong
Won't be too long before they're back
To disappear
And come back again

JUST A NORMAL BOY

Floating up and down
Like I'm falling in the ocean
Letting the waves take me down
Like a hurricane set in motion
Not knowing how to think
I scream aloud, begin to sink
I'm reaching for the life within me
Relaxed and floating into space
Sometimes it feels like I'm falling
Into the ocean
Let the waves take me up and take me down
The hurricane set in motion
I want to swim away but don't know how...

How in the Hell Did You Think I'd Forget-Essay

I am healed by the brothers of, "IN THE MEANTIME."
From them I've learned so much.
I have never spoke about this bad experience. It
involved Marines from the base at Fort Leonard Wood
Maryland Quarters housing. I worked at the hospital.
Nights. 3 PM to 11:45 PM. I was involved in a fight in
the barracks. The fight took place because two
soldiers raped me. I reported the incident seven
months later to Major Rice. While nothing was done to

the men who victimized me, I was moved to another barrack. I then told my Sergeant. He was not any help. So I stayed away from places where I thought I could be raped again. I would only go to church. Then I started going to classes / school and college to suppress the hurt and pain from incident.

In school and college I had many girlfriends but my relationships failed because I felt there were not real. I did not realize I was still upset over the trauma that happened during my time in the military.

I am speaking now about my experiences or how they shaped me as a Black man. At age 70 I feel it is important for me to speak my truth. I also speak for other men who are survivors of rape.

TAMMY
YOUNG

Intro

Even though mother's love flowed, where was the
affection?
Love and affection were replaced with mothers'
expectations.
Female intimacy and connection were quite impacted by
what was missing, but expected.
The fire and touch of another woman, her fire & scent
filled the void.

That's What You Expected!

You expected me to understand why you were not there in
the middle of the night, after a horrible nightmare
That's what you expected!
You expected me to feel safe around all five brothers
That's what you expected!
You expected me to understand why they crept in my bed
at night
That's what you expected!

You expected me to grow up and be all that you could be
That's what you expected!
You expected me to follow all the rules
That's what you expected!
You expected me to know what to do in any situation
That's what you expected!
You expected me to read your mind, sometimes
That's what you expected!
You expected me to go to school or get a job
That's what you expected!
You expected me to have all the right answers
That's what you expected!
Well here's what I expected!
I expected you to show me the way to go

That's what I expected!
I expected you to teach me all the rules
That's what I expected!
I expected you to guide me through any tough situation
That's what I expected!
I expected you to share with me what was on your mind
That's what I expected!
I expected you to tell me to finish school, than get a job
That's what I expected!
I expected you to ask all the right questions
That's what I expected
I expected you to be there and comfort me
That's what I expected!
I expected you to know that five boys going through
puberty, could be a bit much for an only girl/sister/daughter

That's what I expected!
I expected you to believe me when I said this is what they
did when you were gone
That's what I expected!
Now that we know what all the expectations are about, let's
learn to RESPECT what we expected
That's what I'm suggesting, respect, yeah!

Tammy Young April 2011

OBIE FORD III, PHD

An Essay on Coming Out

I'm not sure that I thought it was "different" until I got a little older, like third or fourth grade. I mean, I can remember having crushes on girls but I can also remember having crushes on boys when I was younger. I think my earliest boy crush was second or third grade. As I was getting older, I don't know, there was something in me that knew there were other little boys that felt the same way.

You know what I mean?

I just kinda knew that other boys were going through it. Like, I don't know when I knew "faggot" was something bad. I guess by time I was being called, "faggot," I knew that it hurt. Our society, particularly our community, doesn't make it easy for people to just come out and say, "Hey, I'm gay." It's always expected that you have a girlfriend...that you're with a girl. So, anything different from that must be wrong, I guess.

I came out to myself in junior high, probably sixth or seventh grade. I didn't think it was right. I used to pray every night for being gay to go away. When I was in eleventh grade, maybe twelfth grade, is when I stopped that prayer because I was like, "This isn't going no where. This is it."

I came out to my mom when I was 19 years old. I was a sophomore in college.
I came out to her because she's just my momma. You know what I mean?
My mom and I are really close and it just didn't make sense for her not to know.

I would be going through stuff and wanted to talk to my mom about it. Tell her, ask her advice about something. It was just weird, her not knowing. Now that I think about it, it was completely ridiculous, but it's what I was going through.

I went home one time during spring break and I talked to her. We were having a great time. One evening, she was resting. I went into her room and climbed into bed with her, and I was like, "Mom, I have a situation."

She said, "What?"

I said, "I have a friend who is in love with me and I don't really know how to deal with that."

In my mind, I already knew how to deal with it. I'd already handled it but this was my way to come out to my mother.

And so, I said, "I don't really know how to deal with it. It's not because he's a guy because I'm really into guys. It's just that he's my friend and I really don't know how to handle this situation."

And she said, "Wait a minute. Wait a minute, wait...wait. Back up. Back up...now, say that again."

I said, "Well, it's not that he's a guy, I'm really into guys. It's just that I don't know how to deal with this situation. He's my friend, you know?"

She said, "Now, what did you mean you're into guys like that?"

I said, "I'm into guys like that."

She said, "You're into guys like *that*?"

I said, "I'm into guys like that."

She said, "Okay." She sat up, paused for a second, like she was thinking about it. Then, she said, "Well, here's what you do, baby…"

I interrupted her, and was like, "Here's what I do, about what?"

She was like, "Yes, about your friend who's in love with you. Isn't that what you wanted to talk about?"

I smiled all hard and was like, "Yes ma'am!"

She said, "Okay…"

J. NATHAN PRICE

Poem-Untitled

The sun set low against the blue
giving off a brilliant red hue.
The sky seemed to be ablaze
the perfect ending to an Autumn day.
The leaves clung to the limbs closely
as the first snow gently covered the moss
who's time was coming to an end
from them there'd be no flower or fragrance.
Fall was coming in full glory
with her harsh, but beautiful storyl.
It wasn't enough snow to cover the hill
but one might meet a snowball or feel the chill.
the pond wasn't ready for skate
and one wondered how long one had to wait.
I see here and there a bird on the wing
and ask,"what happened to all the lovely things?

The green meadows are covered now.
The chirp of birds replaced by the hum of snow plows.
The cornfields are stained a battleship gray.
The green leaves have all passed away.
For three months he'll be gone
until the rising of the Spring sun.
But for now I'll enjoy the snowflakes
and all the beauty and symmetry that fall displays.

DAVID JONES

Poem-BLOOD HYMN
(Inspired by a theater piece and by Juba Kalamka, Oakland, California)

Lord, where does your blood flow?
No mortal eye can see my son
And no mortal tongue can tell
It overflows our communion chalices
It writhes and screams, refusing to be contained in our plastic vials
This Blood flows far beyond the Cross
It is on the hands of those who exploit the innocent
It is the Blood that splattered a New York street
Marking the holy place where Sakia Gunn's body lay
It is the Blood oozing out of every gay man
Out of every lesbian in church pews
Cut by "faggot" shrapnel and burnt by "sissy" napalm
It boils in the veins of those who fight for justice
and die for mercy
It is on the sheets of every rape victim whose power is stolen---
that too is My Blood
It is the Blood of HIV victims-----mortal death and Eternal Life
mingling in a thunderous dance------blood killing them, Blood
assuring that they will die no more
This too is my Blood
See that you are not guilty of it
That its flaming Crimson cause your soul and spirit to pause in
its presence
See that you adore it with grateful love
For it is Precious
O the Blood of Jesus
It must not suffer loss

Poem-HOMELAND OF THE SOUL
(DEDICATED TO TRUE BELIEVERS, CHURCH QUEENS AND CHOIR
SISSIES FROM COAST TO COAST. FOR YOU I POUR OUT)

I can't leave
I don't care what that damn professor say
I can't
I won't
This is my father's praying ground
My mother's threshing-floor
Just can't
Yes, I see the bloody choir robes
the pulpit filthy
salt and vinegar
where milk, honey and living bread ought to be
but I can't go
this is my home
My grandma wore this pew out with her trumpeting hallelujahs
I can still hear echoes of her brazen, apocalyptic alto
the raspy edge cutting the vibrating air
"The Lord will Make a way, oooooooohhhhh yes He will"
It is in this exalted choir stand
that I found out my voice was good for more than just talking
and that there was more than one way to speak
It is in the pew across from me
that the man I married first dipped his pen of love in my heart
softly
tenderly
so as to not disturb the homophobia atoms in the air above us
the church
impossibly, inevitably forward
frustratingly, un-movably backward
filled with the children of light
we empty and full all at once
praying for mercy
savoring grace
where the fuck we supposed to go?
Look, I ain't leaving home.
White man's religion my ass
and I KNOWS there is a God
you ain't got shit to replace this with

you want me to go out in the dark
Without the Light of the World?
Nigga, I'm staying home

SALIMA MASUD

Poem-Causes

"gonna lay down my sword and shield down by the
riverside." negro spiritual

soul got tired of pounding dirt,
ducking blows and dogs,
but i marched on.

stretch the legs again,
hoisted a peace sign,
spent a night in jail.

carried a rainbow banner,
kissed sameness on
a street corner in greenwich village.

took up reserved arms,
and stood ready for action,
in heat, sand and fire.

gonna lay down my spark
and kindle before i
reach the stove.

aint't going to study war no more.

BILL ALLEN, JR.

What does the face of 'love' look like?
Would you be able to recognize it, if it
came in plain sight?
If it were not "wrapped" in the covering
that you thought was right;
Would you dismiss its contents and
send it back into that long day's night?
Never knowing what gift, that might have
been brought.
Now denied, lonely, anxious and
distraught;
Look at what you could have had, with
just a little more thought.
                    ----Bill Allen, Jr.

Many times we *think* we know what we're looking for.

Other times, we look for things that just *cannot* be found; regardless of how *hard* we try. On occasions, we stop looking; and what we wanted or *needed* unexpectedly appears. But like adjusting to the weather, you've got to be prepared for whatever may come...or not.

It was unusually cold for that time of year. I could see the shrubs arguing with the leaves from the trees; and the winds hollering back in an orchestrated frenzy. Hardly a romantic night. The uncharitable gusts of air introduced itself to my warm breath. Only a brother with a tight spiritual bond of friendship would come out to support his friend on a night like that. My friend's "gala" event was a good-hearted attempt. Nothing was truly memorable; except one particular person whom had been assigned to my reception table. The "visually captivating, six foot tall, well–defined, dark-chocolate-framed Adonis----was the dessert of the table, as far as I was concerned! His Barry White sounding voice said that he was

Anthony. Worldly but not jaded, his energy co-mingled with my teacher/ performing artist/dancer persona. That night was the start of an eclectic, high-voltage choreographed tango that was to last forever.

Upon leaving from the event, it had started raining. The wet droplets cascading my face were seemingly the joyful tears from the clouds----a sign that I had been given an unexpected gift. Rain would come to symbolize many joys that Anthony and I would share----running in the "wet silver" with our beautiful family cocker spaniel on one side of me and my bronzed ebony knight, with his glistening skin, on my other side. The fresh air was penetrating my lungs with exuberance; and my eyes blinked with the moisture of love. When coming from dancing almost all night at Jewell's Catch One Disco, it has been sprinkling and the wet pavement made Anthony and I look like a moving collage under the flickering and shimmering lights. We became an ode to night's magic.

We celebrated culinary gifts that we'd both create and surprise each with; and invite best friends over to share in being grateful to "break bread together." There were dinners at "artiste cafes;" We'd always toast to celebrate "something new." There were visits to our best friend Patricia and staying 'til almost dawn. The Three Musketeers we had become. Onto concerts and picnics at the Greek Theatre too; feeling as if Johnny Mathis and Dionne Warwick were singing only to our friend and us two. Feasts would be created by me for the holiday times.

Much to be grateful for and acknowledging that our life was blessedly divine.

But then the weather changed. Thunder clapped "that the clear skies would end." Doctors, hospitals, procedures and pills would begin. Was this to be "the end of our beginning ...or the beginning of the end?" If I didn't know... the weather sure did; for a change was approaching---- the blowing an ill-wind.

The day morosely came----when I had my own "emotional earthquake." Anthony *ordered* me to *leave* and go home...as he was preparing to go *home*. In leaving the hospital, I morosely lumbered under the overcast sky's *stinging* rain---- while angry and anguished tears pelted me with an inconsolable pain of loss. I stepped along the symbolic debris of my life. I didn't know how to focus on even getting out of the parking lot; for my eyes were glazed with grief. Glaring lights blinded into the wet pavement, creating "unstable collages of faceless people," who could *never* cry for you. But the rain always would. Many people's "concerns" would wash down the drain----like the rain. And I would have to learn how to move on, whether rain...or shine.

After Anthony, I became an "island" unto myself. After three years, I re-joined society, but only encountered "chipped and sharp edges" of men too wounded to give; or gave only what they could wound. My work became my new mistress. I taught youth and young adults how to value themselves; to value getting knowledge; and to value how to stay healthy in mind, body and soul. I choreographed and wrote productions----that addressed the signs of the times. AIDS, classism, racism, sexism and all other "isms," that our world looked at; with eyes that were blind. And in time, I learned that you overcome the loss of a love----by giving of your talents and abilities...*with* more love. An old Black saying of "folk wit" once told us---- "Tell me whom you love, and I'll tell you who you are." Well, I have the face of a man, who has been loved. And now I try to heal our wounded people----with words of hope, words of joy and words of *love*.

I'M BAFFLED-BILL ALLEN, JR.

How could you reach me so meaningfully, so deeply and so
emphatically----
with such a light ethereal touch?
A touch that unbeknownst to me would come to mean so
much.
A touch that was thousands of miles away; yet, it Fed Exed
itself to the aorta of my heart.
And with its special delivery, it sure didn't miss its mark.
But yet, I'm baffled.
How did you know where to aim your sweet love juices of
penetrating tenderness?
Putting my emotions into a state of undress.
So that the residue was dripping from my woolly hair,
down my wide nose,
My sensuous lips, right on down to my heavy-laden forest
of my tree.
This was having a light-headed, heated effect on me.
Continuing to drip down the ski slopes of my inner thighs,
only to form a warm puddle, right before my eyes

CLAUDIA MOSS

Short Story-Since Talk Walked?

I brought her home to answer the wonderings that drifted
about the family like lost queries seeking responses. Is she
or isn't she? Could it yet be a phase, if she's in her forties?
Did being married to him turn her against all men?
Wonder if the right man, i.e. the one from her adolescence,
the one about whom she reminisces from time to time,
wonder if he could charm her back to The Great Acceptable
Way if they reunited?

To quall their musings and to bodaciously honor self, I did,
in my honest estimation, the kindest thing for all
concerned. I invited her to a Fourth of July celebration at
my sister?s beautiful home in Montgomery, AL. There was
no preamble. There wasn't a foreword. Nor was there a
leak to peak their curiosity. Nothing. Outside of our quasi-
late arrival on a sun-drenched, lazy-hazy sort of day, when
the air snapped fresh and clean and softly invited my
Tuskegee and Auburn family members to fling off their
picnic garb, and don swimwear to cannonball into the
ceramic lushness of Sista Gyrl's cerulean waves.

She and I strolled up the long drive as if they were awaiting
us. Our smiles met them before our spry greetings. Yes, I
knew what we looked like, if the naked curiosity in other
people?s eyes could be translated into much outside of,
"Oh, dykes?" We were the perfect manifestation of the
masculine and the feminine, the rough and the soft, the
painted and the unpainted. Her rakish quality dared
overlooking. It arrested you. Unabashedly. And I adored
her.

Adored her uncanny comedic sense of making me howl,
just fall down laughing, that intelligent, witty delivery of
hers that made her appealing to me in countless, unnamable
ways. I?d heard folks say it for years, but this time I

believed it: If people can make you laugh, they possess the keys to your joy! She said I was hairy. Said her mother said if a girl was hairy, her blood must be rich. And she even claimed to like the ever-so-slight mustache above my upper lip, which I learned to trim to almost nothing before travelling to Hawaii to attend an all-girl wedding on the beach of the Big Island.

My poetry excited her when we first met. Perhaps because I---at one time---performed erotic poetry while arrayed in sensual plumage. Her gaze softened discernibly whenever she saw me, same as it does now if our paths converge.

Together, we greeted my quietly transfixed family, who smiled curious yet warm and friendly hellos while I made my way through the swathe of introductions. This is my father and my stepmother. My sis-in-law and her two angels. And over here are my baby sister's two darlings. Stand up, Sweet Pea. Say hello. No, don't hide your pretty face! That's it, Man! Always speak up, but know when to shut up, too! Who has the grill puffin, people? And on it went, until everyone had been introduced to our warm guest, and she had graced each one with a royal smile that outshined the Royal Couple's blissful kiss yesterday.

Then I disappeared inside the house, leaving her to swim alone in what could have been shark- infested waters had perception weighed a tad bit to the left or to the right. But she was who she was, and I who I was.

Inside, hiding from the tremendous heat, were the women. My stepmother, my sisters, my sister-in-law, and my nieces. Their questions polished the kitchen air. Curiosity thrived alongside heaping platters of buttered corn and pans of baked beans and tossed salad. In a peaceful atmosphere, I bowed to the inquisition. Outside, she charmed the inquest. And when I eventually returned to her side to determine how she was coming along, I was the one standing on the outside of a circle charged with testosterone and smoke and loud laughter. Tickled, I waved and about-faced it on back into the air-conditioned house.

Before the day curtsied to evening, most had the unmitigated gall to third-degree me on whether or not I'd fixed her a plate and made certain her drink was replenished. They tickled me. Later, she and I took the little people for a walk about my sister's cul-de-sac. Joyous, tiny hands locked, they trailed us like we were a Piped Piper pairing and a bit later into the evening, I trailed her, too, as the music of her stories and commentary and laughter rendered me indubitably charmed.

The experience reminded me to embrace talk when it took a notion to walk and walk it out to its healing ending. So many times a destination doesn't have to be disagreeable, when you walk towards it in truth and boldness.

ROBIN G. WHITE

POEM-EXEGESIS

At 13 I knew
More than anything
Or anyone
Who and What
I was.
I knew...
Could barely articulate it,
But I found
The words.

Dug from the back of the Catholic Church
Basement flea market,
I insisted
The old Sylvania
Should be mine.
"That old thing"
Taught me more
Than anything
Or anyone
Who and What
I was.

Secretly ensconced
Under pale pink percale sheets
And heavy cream colored blankets
I listened
To the crackling
Of my radio
A transport
To another time and place.
Here I "rediscovered"
Sarah, Ella, Duke, Billie, Byrd.
Here I listened
Like the grownups did

To the old AM stations
Which played no pop music
Harbored no rock and roll,
But offered up old jazz and swing,
Delivered and discussed
In monotone reverence.
And on Sunday evenings
Played live performances
From some old jazz club
In Downtown Boston.

And so it was
On one
Autumn Sunday evening
Hidden under
The pretty perfection
Of pink sheets
With matching shams
And the downy warmth
Of my cotton duvet
I found the words
Uttered from her lips
Rich words articulated
In ways I couldn't imagine.
She spoke truths
Said things
I knew at 13
Mother would never approve of.
I turned the volume down
Pulled the blanket tighter over my head
Pressed my ear to the dial
And listened
As Pat Parker
Gave me the words
To tell my story.

Pat Parker, Born Patricia Cooks, January 20, 1944 in Houston, Texas; died June 4, 1989. Fierce black lesbian poet, published five volumes and one recording of poetry all by the age of 45 when she died of breast cancer. Parker lived unapologetically black, lesbian and mother. It was through her work and in her words that at 13 I truly found my voice and understood for the first time that I was not alone.

ESSAY-REVELATION

I sat frozen in the back seat unable to move. Getting out of that vehicle would forever change life as I knew it and I wasn't ready. I breathed, pushed one leg out and then the other emerging like a butterfly from the 46-year-old chrysalis which held all my former secrets. I moved toward her and awaited the explosive transformation as every previous second of every previous day dissipated when her arms wrapped around me. I was home.

My mother was an 18-year-old foster child when she had me. Her Irish mother's indiscretion with a black man and death at childbirth had left her alone in the world. At 17 she found love with my father and then me, a five-pound brown-skinned bundle of joy taken by the state until she could put down roots. There was nothing in her life to prepare her for the Brazilian and African-American couple who would take this love from her and keep it hidden until it could find its way home some 46 years later.

There hadn't been a time during those years that I hadn't wondered about her what she was like, what she would think of me. I am a writer, a musician, a lover of children, food and women. I wondered how I came to all of these things: nature vs. nurture. Was I born this way or was it taught? Did someone else in my family have these hips? Was I the only one who could sing? Write? Did others love languages and the way words roll from the soul to the tip of a tongue?

Was my lesbianism informed in some way by the lack of a close mother identity? I couldn't help but wonder as did my therapist, family and even an occasional lover. I sought women with strong family and mother bonds and later with similar cultural identities – strong black or Latina women with strong black or Latina mothers. I longed to connect in some way to what I expected my mother might be: resilient, intellectual and loving, an older version of me. Eventually, I repaired the relationships with both my adoptive and step mothers and still seeking elusive answers I tentatively began the journey toward finding my birth mom.

The phone rang at 11:45 PM. The voice on the other end sounded like my own. "I know you," she said, her audible smile cracking open the door to my hidden life. We laughed and cried and shouted, 'Oh my God,' so many times you would have thought Jesus Himself would show up.

"I knew if you were a Young, you would be up," my sister said explaining a piece of my puzzle. "We are all night owls." I gave that a moment of thought. 'We,' she had said. My family, my father who I shared with her, Cecelia, my little sister, my uncles, aunts and cousins - there were uncles, aunts and cousins. I had more siblings to meet and nieces and nephews to spoil.

"We need to call Mom," she giggled excitedly. Mom and our younger sister would be home from work by now.

"Wait a second," I whispered.

My heart was pounding in my chest. It could be all over before it even started, but with my partner of eight years in the bedroom down the hall I couldn't. I had to ask. I had to tell it. Anything less would be to deny who she was to me or who I was after 33 years of being an out and proud lesbian writer and activist.

After 33 years of working through the issues with my adoptive and step families, I had to put it right out there up front. "There is something I need to tell you," I said sheepishly. Oh, God. Suppose they were born-again Christians. "I'm a lesbian," I said and waited.

"Ho ho!" she laughed. Laughed! "I wondered when you said you weren't married and didn't have kids. I wondered if you had that gene."

"What?" I didn't understand.

"Yeah, Mom and our sister are too!" It took a second for what she was saying to sink in. And then there it was the revelation, the answer to that question. It was in my genes plain and simple. All of the worries went away. All of the years of fighting for who I was and who I loved had been vindicated. The activism, the losses, the gains all of it...I was right where I was supposed to be as I was supposed to be.

A month later after a very moving Miami airport reunion between me and Cecelia, sleep swept over me during the three-hour ride to Key West where our mom and youngest sister lived. I watched Cecelia move out of the car and then my partner, who turned around to coax me along. In that moment, all of the years of fear, pain and sadness were a newborn veil I pushed aside to embrace my life and my new understanding of it. I moved toward her and felt for the first time my mother's loving embrace. Yes. I finally was home.

SWAY
1.
Daddy sways
Mesmerized by horns blaring
Staccato chords chopping rhythms
Through the air.
"That's the heart beat.
Feel it. Right
There. Right
There. Right
Here,"
His fingers tap my chest in
Synco-pa-tion.
I am aloft.
Tiny Mary Janes
On large shiny black Florsheims.
Byrd, Ellington, Miles
Defining our movements
Till the needle runs out of vinyl.
The arm releases another
And Daddy is again transformed
Dizzy, Getz
Gilberto, Puente, Rivera
Daddy's hips speak another language
One I lovingly come to know.
Samba, salsa, merengue,
"It's all in the hips," he says
As my family quietly chuckles
At the five-six-seven-eight-nine-year-old nonexistence.
"She has no hips."
"I have hips; don't I Daddy."
"Yes, Pumpkin. You have hips."
Until I am ten,
I lose myself with my father in Brazil.
I will live there forever.

2.
"How do you do that?"
First the white girls question
Then the black
As Donna belts out Hot Stuff
While Barry, Maurice and Robin
Croon If I Can't Have You.
My curvaceous hips articulate rhythms
Unknown to our seemingly cloistered
Provincial Brahmin aristocracy.
I become the woman with the hips
As I tongue and finger my way
Across stages
My flute
Beating out Cuban and Brazilian rhythms
Naturally
In time with
The words of
My heart.

3.
"It's a rhythm," I say,
An art form.
Cabinet to pot
Pot to sink
Sink to fridge
Fridge to counter
Counter to stove
And back again.
The movement punctuated
With flourishes of color
And scents artfully awakening
Some deep Latin spirit.
I divine culinary concoctions
Prophetically moving diners to tears.
Arms in motion

The graceful salsa dancer
Fluid, swaying
An unearthly magic
In the kitchen.
It is the heart.
Lovingly in motion
Singing joys
Into ambrosial distractions.

4.
"I AM Gumbo," I say.
The revelation
Hovering in my brain.
Irish, French, Caribbean, Creole,
Spanish Jew, Seminole and Blackfoot
Among other things
All stirred in a Brazilian pot.
My mother's and father's mother's
Dowry behind me.
I now am keenly aware
Of the origins of my unique dance,
A beautiful rhythm
I lovingly embrace.
Mambo, Merengue, Salsa, Samba, Step
Dutty Wine, Capoeira, Funk;
It is all right
Here.
I stir with long-handled spoons,
Cook the long-ago divination
Of my ancestors,
Burn the pots,
Put my foot in it,
Reach back to pantries
Full of understanding;
Wisdom gathers in the kitchen:
I AM finally home.

Paquito D'Rivera plays.
I am transformed.
Watch my sway.

RENAIR AMIN

Poem-Shhh (Listen)

Shhh...
Close your eyes and listen to the sounds of the anguish
Can you hear the wishes of those who cry through their
soul
Across state lines
Into times when love wasn't enough
And living was too tough
The teen who flees fearfully with tears in his eyes
wondering why he
Thought like this
Looked like this
Never wanted to French kiss a girl
And only liked to twirl in frilly things
Putting on his mother's rings
And her other personal things
Or the young lesbian who shakes her head as she wraps her
hands around the strands of cloth
Trying to approximate how late it would be before her
parents would check
And find her swinging to the tocks of her death
Emotionally bruised and needing to leave this earth to all
its hurt
Or the young couple that would cry together as they held
each other
Smothered in thoughts of how they could never marry
No legacy to carry
Just two more abominations of creation within this nation
Signing the lines on the suicide pact
Just drafted with the blood still adapting to the paper
Stationed in a world where it's better to hurl slurs and fists
Than to uplift and wish them well
Hell hath no fury like a soul scorned
Only willing to burn themselves
Because the perpetrators are more than just peer haters and

the problem is greater than this
Whispers of Rest In Peace posted on Facebook walls and
text crawls
It's hard for me because
I remember sitting and watching the blood as it flowed
down my arm from self mutilation
Later hating those bottles of pills that would spill leaving
my mouth charcoal black
And stomach pumped nearby stacks of papers filled out
with a diagnosis of attempted suicide
Yet I remember more time with razors savoring no longer
living
Giving God ultimatums
If only he would stop saving me
I would stop living
Lying to friends and family as my brain turned tragically
Until one day the pain was too severe
I truly feared not the actual leaving but the mechanism by
which I was scheming
So I called them
The "them" with the white jackets and hooks
Who came with stoic looks as they had seen this before
And there was more
Because I had been on the floor for 3 days
With no desire to yell for help
Just wanted another way to remove myself
But it was holding the gun that taught me that my insanity
wasn't wanting to die
It was the inability to love internally
But this story is not about me or is it
Farther than just some hospital visit
More hits than some internet widget
Just a smidgen of reality mixed in with these tragedies
And compassion is necessary
Especially when many times we can be blind to what is
really going on

So when someone calls you singing their song
Don't change the melody into a chorus

Please

Keep your eyes closed and listen to the sounds of the
anguish
Can you hear the pleas of those that cry through their soul
Don't you understand
This wasn't part of my plan
How can I stand when my world is flat
I am sailing to fall off
Because I am the one being scoffed at
Flaunted and laughed at
Stabbed at
Broadcasted that I am not like them
And when it's no longer funny
They just push and shove me
Physically and emotionally
Can u explain how this can be my life
Can you explain to me how this is right

People

That is the mentality dims their light
With no right answers to find
No time to unwind
Sometimes we look with sight not seeing
Hear with ears missing meaning
Tears in eyes gleaming
Or even non-existent
Let's create role models in places where happy is missing
Change the paradigm
Find time to chat with a person that we normally wouldn't
Take time from teaching to be a student
Be a safe haven where your behavior may be their savior

Or just good favor
And if someone can't hear you
Don't take it personal but do everything to withstand so you
can stand with your hand out

And

For those who can't breathe
And each time you inhale
Your colors pale until you're axed out and only hell reigns
Hear me when I say this pain will subside
Even when there is nowhere to hide
Find someone to talk to
To console you when you feel a halt to your life is the only
way
Today
When weeping may be enduring for a night
There is joy in the morning
Even when in this second you may be mourning
Wondering where to go
How to know
When there is no one to tell you so
And the rainbow isn't enough
It's just another reason you feel rebuffed
Life is more just failing chances
Relationships broken and failed trances
Things do pass sometimes get better
Even when the tear-stained tissues get wetter and wetter

So

Let us all join hands and stand for each other
Sisters and brothers
Community linking
Consoling mothers and strong fathers
Give birth to a movement

Where we become units
United
To bring them out alive
We must let bygones be by bygones
And show we can survive
And while we are stationed in a world where it seems better
to hurl slurs and fists
Let us be the ones to encourage, support and uplift

COLE THOMAS

AKA

AGENDA BENDA JUSTICE

Cole E. Thomas
The Intriguing AGgressive
AGenda Benda Justice, Founder
AGendaBendaGear, CEO

What I know so far

Citizen activists, black women.
Queer, black women.
Mothers, black women.
We appear united and organized, but are we?

People of faith. Spiritually enlightened, black women
led to trust the God of our own understanding.
Those of limited means. One subsection of black
women.
Artists. Black women of an even smaller community.
We offer support and encouragement, but do we truly
deliver?

Students and teachers, black women.
Entrepreneurs and consumers, black women.
Leaders, mediators, and crew, black women.
We intellectualize the formula for success and self-
actualization,
but can we implement and execute with authenticity?

Yes. No. Sometimes.
No. Yes. Sometimes.
Sometimes, Yes. Sometimes, No.

When we are able to examine the parts of us, as well
as the whole from which these parts are made,
We find that though we share traits and
characteristics,
We are diverse, dynamic, and ever-shifting...
Just like other human groups.

Those of us with the ability, the means, and the reach
help us to community-build.
Those with the ability, the means, *or* the reach help us
to community-build.
Those with neither ability, means, nor reach begin as
soldiers, as students.

When we look to only to ourselves, we may languish.
When we look only to others, we might languish still.
Systematic collaboration is that pot of gold at the ends
of our rainbows that seems to consistently elude us.
Is it that we have not yet, as queer, African American
black women, socially and economically evolved
To the point that we can withstand a loss or failure if a
large-scale collaboration fails?
Do we pervasively mistrust, suspecting one another of
ulterior motives;
Or are we simply overwhelmed with negative
reactions to all the layers?

- minority
- minority
- minority
- minority
- minority
- minority
- minority
- minority

Can we not find the space, the energy in our lives for
networking and resource development?
If so, we must involve more minds and bodies, and
then each take on smaller chunks.

Kinship, sharing and camaraderie prove vital to

foundation-building.
Distrust isn't inherently problematic; *mistrust is*.
(A system based upon distrust simply introduces
checks and balances within power structures.)
Is this our missing piece?
Our future lies in building sturdy organizations and
lasting alliances,
Businesses and institutions that encourage us to live
our best lives, authentically.

Moving forward this agenda by modeling courage
through connection seems my purpose these days.
When we truly grow, we shed some things and people
we've held dear ,
And we need to be met with empathy and guidance
during these transitions!
Walking with others in the lesbian, gay, bisexual,
transgender, intersex, queer, and questioning
communities,
Who try to balance income-earning and personal
wellness with fulfilling their roles in the lives of others
Defines us as a community of substance and
compassion.

Certainly seems odd that we lose things as we
become stronger.
Patience and perseverance allow us to see that the
painful or frightening impact of letting go, is
temporary.
If not, it becomes manageable the more closely we
walk together in our faiths.
The gifts, though - *both the ones we give and receive*
- are beyond our wildest expectation.

Citizen activists, black women.
Queer, black women.

Mothers, black women.
United and organized.

People of faith. Spiritually enlightened, black women
led to trust the God of our own understanding.
Those of limited means. One subsection of black
women.
Artists. Black women of an even smaller community.
Supported and encouraged.

Students and teachers, black women.
Entrepreneurs and consumers, black women.
Leaders, mediators, and crew, black women.
Successful and self-actualized.

Connecting is what I do.
I use my voice, my talents, my wisdom, my muscle,
my prayers, my influence
My love
So that other women like me might do the same.
This is what I know so far.

*And those last five "minority" bullets up there?
They are "shouts out" bullets:
One is for the impoverished among us. One is for my
butch/boi/stud tribe. One is for multiracial and black
biracial SLG sisters.
One is for our other-abled family.
The last is for the lesbian sisters and trans family in
and from those countries on the African continent who
still fear imprisonment or execution as a consequence
for being discovered.

DEE RENEE SMITH

Poem-We Are Love

I am an offspring
of religious upbringings.
Generations of tradition drilled
into the foundation
of our spiritual homes
until stunted roots
left our base distorted
from the abuse.

I am from
a family of spiritualists.
A lineage of spirit movers.
Holders of God's hand,
yet, not courageous enough
to keep religion
out of our blood line.

I am a child of God
though I feel too weak
at times to say it.
For so long, I've known it
but I didn't feel it.
There's been too much fear.

I was raised by fear.
Disciplined by fear
and encouraged by fear.
In this type of caution
and constant pausing
to analyze the possibility
of punishment for just being,

I never really understood
what loving God was about.

For the first time, this week,
I feel loved by God.
For years, I've been loved
and never said thank you
to God and many folks
because I feared they would be
repulsed or as fearful as I was
about the possibility that love
could just be a consistent part of life
and of them.

I am thankful for growth
and for love's constant nature.
I am thankful that it never changes
for the embodiment of love
exists infinitely.
In innumerable units
of any measurement of being

and just as love is
I thank God right now
that I am love
and I love God
right now as I am.

GALE SKY

EDEAWO

Short Story-Jenny & Jolene

"Jenny, don't keep sitting there woman. You're going to freeze waiting here thinking you can keep warm whenever the underground subway passes by and blows warm air through the steam grate. I can't understand why you continue sitting in this doorway, feeling cold and looking dumb, while we have a three bedroom apartment we are leasing just around the corner. I left there to come searching for you. I made a big pot of beef stew and left it simmering on the stove. You know you have always loved my beef stew. Got Dinah Washington blowing on the stereo, and I just added some wood to the fireplace."

Jolene moved closer to Jenny who was sitting idle on a bundle of rags and pleaded, "Jenny, please come in from the cold. I am seriously beginning to worry about your mental health. Is your condition the one they call Alzheimer, I believe you're too young for that, or are you entering early senility? Or maybe you are just plain crazy." The word CRAZY brought Jenny back to reality just in time to realize that there was less heat rising from the steam grate, and if she didn't do something very soon she was going to freeze just like Jolene warned. Jenny began to think that perhaps she was really going crazy, and maybe that explained why she kept walking away from the warm, loving home she had shared for twenty years with her best friend Jolene.

Jenny and Jolene had many things in common. They were both medium weight and height, attractive dark brown skinned women with laughing eyes and pleasing smiles. Both enjoyed the same blues songs and jazz divas, they also enjoyed the same movies, books and food. They even had affectionate nicknames for one another. Jolene called Jenny "Too Tan", and Jenny called Jolene "Velvet." No one was surprised when they leased a three bedroom apartment within walking distance to their job at the factory and set up housekeeping together.

They met in their mid thirties while working the assembly line on the graveyard shift. The dead man's shift they jokingly called it. Within two years, Jolene, who worked harder than any man, worked her way up to lead supervisor and was transferred to the day shift. Jenny who was also ambitious took business courses at the local college and later became a manager at the factory. Neither of them had children, so the money they made between them was quite agreeable with their lifestyle.

They found themselves living out their dreams. Both of them took trips every year. They often went home to visit family; home being Louisiana for Jenny, and Michigan for Jolene. Other times they vacationed in exotic places such as Hawaii, Mexico, or Jamaica. Sometimes they traveled with groups and other times alone with each other.

Parties at the house were regular. Quite a few of the factory workers moved in their inner circle and took turns having card parties, dinners and anniversaries, at one another's home. There were competitive bowling tournaments, birthday parties and semi annual Atlantic City turn-about trips. Life at that time was very good, full of warmth, love, and happiness. They had a feeling of serenity, a security of which no one in their circle hoped would ever end.

All continued to go well until four years ago when the factory closed down. For years there had been warning signs, and a few temporary lay-offs, but the workers were always called back, and production went on as usual. Not even was the management staff prepared for what was about to happen. They were given twenty four hours to inform all employees of the immediate shut-down. Rumor later had it that the factory relocated to a small southern town, or moved across the border to Mexico where labor was much cheaper. These moves did not include Jenny or Jolene. Nearly 95% of the factories working staff was left jobless.

After their jobs terminated, life was not easy for them. Both had small savings tucked away, but when their un-employment benefits ran out they went though their savings rapidly. Employers were not quick to hire women over fifty, no matter what their past experiences were. Resumes were hand carried, sent by mail, and sent by fax, to no avail.

They also learned, too soon, that the recession had forced many businesses out of existence, or left them no choice other than to freeze hiring or cut cost. It was 1996 and a totally new world had built up around their once very secure status. Until the truth kicked in they had never took a look at what lied ahead of them. They were both unprepared for the reality of the future.

Jenny slowly looked up into Jolene's concerned face, a face that was once so smooth and velvet, now was deeply lined with worry as she gathered Jenny's personal belongings from the steam grate and placed them in a large plastic bag while complaining about how desperately they needed laundering. "Jenny," Jolene said as she broke into Jenny's thoughts "Why are you living like this? I am beginning to worry about your behavior. Hiding out in doorways, sitting on piles of rags, wearing filthy clothes, and protecting this area as if it were a fortress. We are not homeless yet, so stop behaving as if we were."

Jenny finally spoke as she pulled herself to a standing position, "You're right Jolene, maybe there is something wrong with my thinking. My mind has been playing tricks on me ever since I had that mild stroke last spring. I think I had better make an appointment at the new mental health facility that recently opened up downtown. I hear they do great work there, and It's also free." Jolene dropped everything she was doing and made a sudden turn to face Jenny. "Stop talking nonsense. You're just moody right now and a bit depressed. Old as you are it is probably just your menopause cycle finally kicking in." It always made Jenny smile when Jolene made statements about menopause because Jolene was a woman who claimed to be born into this world going the menopause, and had finished her cycle by age fifteen. She also swore that she had medical papers to prove it. Of course no one ever saw the papers. Jolene took Jenny by the hand and said "What you really need is a stiff shot of brandy and we'll phone some friends to drop by the house. Come on honey, let's go home. The brandy is waiting. We'll invite some of our buddies over to play cards, watch sports on T.V. and see who can outlie, out laugh and out dance the others.

The two women walked arm and arm down the cold street. Jolene pushed Jenny's cart while verbally preparing her for the great activities in store for them that evening. It will be just like old times. Jolene climbed the six steps that led to the stoop leading to their apartment, pulling the cart behind her as Jenny lifted the opposite end. They opened the front door and entered their warm modest domain.

"Now isn't this better?" Jolene asked as she affectionately looked at Jenny. "It damn sure is," Jenny replied. "Now bring me some of that simmering stew I'm smelling." "In a minute honey," Jolene assured her. "First let's hear us some Dinah Washington and hold each other close." Jenny poured two small glasses of brandy, while Jolene turned up the volume on the stereo.....

Across the street two younger women were observing Jenny and Jolene from there front window. "There go those two crazies", one of the younger women sadly said to the other. "They have run off from the Women's Shelter again. Just to come and sit in that cold vacant lot where their apartment building once stood. I fear that one day they may freeze to death out there. Call the shelter," she ordered her friend, "let them know that they are here again, it is the least we can do."

Turning away from her friend, the young woman continued focusing her attention on the two women across the street. They both appeared very happy, laughing and dancing around a steel barrel which contained a lukewarm fire. The young woman thought fearfully to herself, "If this economy does not improve soon, and my roommate and I don't find employment, we will be forced to join those women." The younger women had already been issued a 60 day notice letting them know that their building would soon be demolished, to make way for some new development. "There but for the Grace of God," the younger woman thought as she turned sadly away from the window....

As the evening grew colder and the sun began to set, Jenny and Jolene continued to amuse themselves in the apartment that was no longer there, sipping on drinks that only they could taste; dancing to music that only their ears could hear.....

KATRINA ARANGO

Essay-Making Love In Heaven

Nothing stands between us. Absolutely nothing. I'm inside you and you're inside me. The allness of me vibrates, starting from the deep center of my core and it reaches into you. This sensation is pure joy. A joy so profoundly intense no human expression would ever come close to describing it. It is more like joy, love and erotic delirium all wrapped into one magnetic force, which draws you further into my depths. And I into yours. I see all that you ever were and all that you ever will be.

There is no beginning to you, nor an end, only YOU. Your form has been all colors, shapes, sizes and genders. But still, I see only YOU. I feel only YOU, as I've always done since we split off at our very creation. The enormity and vastness of our love is all encompassing and the impact of our spirits against and into one another's produces a piercing, blissful light so brilliant that the illuminated echoes can be seen from across the universe.

Being one with you is like coming into myself, yet falling into us as a one. It's as if you never left me but I've felt the absence of you over decades, centuries, millennia. An array of celestial colors, never known to the human eye, pulsate and flow through us like beams of ardor. They intensify and move like waves of unstable gravity, pulling and pushing us together until finally the music of our souls begin to sync, like one perfect orchestra. The sound of it, so beautiful and divine, permeates our very beings. And we are one.

Poem-Black Wine

Pour me up a glass of that wine
And please, only the black kind
I crave drops of Nubian sweetness
Upon my lips tasting so divine
Black wine smooth and warm
Caressing the insides of me
Totally and completely
My own dark retreat
Lips that are full and moist
Sweet, black berries playing in my mouth
Tongues dancing and flying into a frenzy
Like the beat of the African drums of the South
Fingers, curls, dred locs, chocolate-hued skin against
Caramel sugar and easy intoxication
Coming together like the richness of mother earth
The beauty of this oneness has immeasurable worth
Black wine going down slow
Into the place where life begins
To love me there is never a sin
Offering myself at the altar of your love
Lifting my glass up high
As I watch black liquid love shining
And reflecting in your brown eyes
Let it flow, sensual and free, over my brown flesh
Ripe and luscious and bursting
Dark droplets of juice saturate fingers and tongues
Sucking, licking, slowly savoring
Devouring
Intoxicating
Black wine
Only this will do
This Nubian fruit which calls and beckons my soul
Satisfies me at my core
Always leave me wanting more

Black wine is what I adore
Black wine belongs to me forevermore

Poem-Til' We Meet Again

Sometimes I find you, and sometimes you find me
It's always the same
A joy so profound it spans through the centuries
One look into YOU
And I can see US
Fragments of time broken down
minutes, years, era's of time like rust
A connection we began at the start of it all
Always circling back into one another
Learning, loving, growth big or small
When I hear the sound of Mozart in my ear
I see visions of you dancing close
whispering elegant prose and sweet words
as you press me ever so near
Standing at the edge of the shore
as the moon light caresses my flesh
the salt air mixed with your tragic kiss
is what I recall best
The smell of a crackling fireplace
as the sun fades to black
snow falling, children laughing
Might be poor but love makes up the lack
Floating down the river Nile
Golden palms gently fan your face
I am your loyal servant and secret lover
As you guide and lead a great race
African hands torn apart
we painfully meet our fate
wails escape our throats
the new world impatiently awaits
New Years Eve rooftop romance
the sky glitters and glows

It's 1920 and glamour is aplenty
My clandestine affair with the star of the movie show
Smoke filled jazz club
you show off in your sharp suit
twirling me and dipping me
Tonight I'm looking like sweet fruit
Every time you promise with spoken word
"Don't be sad, because this will never end"
for you'll search for your eternal flame forevermore

As you kiss my lips and say "Til' we meet again"

IFALADE TASHIA ASANTI

AMERICA DON'T KNOW TRUE LOVE-FOR PEPPER
(11/18/2004)

america don't know true love
let me introduce you

love is the smile on her lips

that breathes life back into my Blackness

when I'm feeling like it would be easier to be white today

love is her faith in my poetry

long before it ever appeared in Essence Magazine

love is the rhythm she drummed back into my heart

when my heart was begging God to let it stop and rest...

love is the ten million times she took my hand in the darkness
that you left me in
and guided me back to myself

love is the living room she sacrificed

so that i could build a railroad in the form of a shrine

so that we could get to Africa from my basement

i said america don't know love, it couldn't

if america knew love it could see the dozens of graves i dug for
myself

the midnights she uncovered me

turned your dirt into medicine to cleanse my spirit with

if america knew love it would see all the men she died for

so they could be reborn again

if America knew true love it wouldn't condemn her
it would demonize the fathers that tried to imprison her right
to grow up and be

america would count all the days she called in sick

just cuz she knew one of our soldiers/me

needed to see her an extra hour

cuz if i couldn't smell her skin

i might give up on the land of the free

become an ancestor before my time

and if i wrote a thousand poems in one hour

i couldn't poetize or realize

the sacrifices she's offered to the altar of my human condition

america, i tell you, you can't know true love
if you did, the vibration of her hours upon hours of chanting

nam-myoho-renge-kyo

would've moved america to engage in world peace

instead of financing this war against brown people, native
people, asian people, latino people and jewish people

hell, it's a war against all her people

cuz america don't know love!

love can't be found on the rotting pages of a constitution

written by colonized pens
love can't be defined by the sons of former slave owners who
do vodou in the basement of yale university & preach morality
on CNN
love can't be recreated by men that seek to rewind history and
reincarnate the next third world holocaust

love ain't written on the pages of a religion that america stole
from egypt
and plagiarized for the rule of a patriarchal society

america's true love is here
right here
standing before you on so-called sinner's feet

america's love is in between morning kisses and good night
hugs
between women or men or any two humyns

america's love is in me and my mate's longevity
on the waves of our laughter
dancing on the ocean of our joy
in the memories and full bellies of our grandchildren

america's love was born the day of our commitment ceremony
in the sweat lodge
on the winds of oya

the womb of oshun
in the wisdom of the buddhas

we are the sanctity of marriage

indigenous and pure

completely undeniable

and today i crown her with the holiest words that a pen could
conjure
before the sacred audience of the poet
i invoke the silence of zora neale hurston to speak now from
my lips

zora, who loved dozens of women
and was never photographed with one

i call forth the power of the duality of bessie smith
bessie: the jazz queen who refused to sing in a skirt

i spit this libation for bayard rustin
the gay man that formed the footsteps for the march on
montgomery
and all the children who hide their love
because they are afraid america will see it
on this day i say to the earth

i love her

and that what we have
is one of the truest loves
that god ever made

in america

www.tashiaasanti.com

MARCI

HALILI

AKOMA

Short Story-Dance

Dance is Dedicated with love and undying devotion to my beloved, Kathy Halili Akoma
With whom I always hope to dance…..

The couple danced underneath the sparkling lights of the hotel's holiday display. People were coming and going, cars pulling into and out of the busy parking lot. Horns were honking, doors slamming, keys jangling. The soft Spanish of the attendants was carrying across the asphalt. The couple danced as if they were all alone in the world. They had been there for hours, not bothered by the chilling winds that picked up and swirled leaves around their legs. As they spun and dipped and swayed they looked lovingly into one another's eyes softly crooning old-fashioned love songs.

They were two middle aged African women, dressed in the colors and fabrics of the motherland. The taller of the two was solidly built with soft, graying locks surrounding her beautiful black face. The other woman was slender, her curly afro wildly framing sparkling eyes in a light brown face.

The teenagers came out of the crowded movie theater, bouncy with youthful energy and enthusiasm. The girl reached for the hand of the young man she called her boyfriend.

"Aww Shorty" he said, pulling quickly away.

"You know I don't roll like that. But, I'll give you something to hold onto later tonight" he leered.

Imani sighed, trying to hide her hurt and disappointment. She had given her virginity to Kwame almost 6 months ago. But despite regular sexual athletics they had never shared a tender or gentle moment. She wished she could be more like the girls on her favorite music videos. Those girls never seemed to want anything as corny as hand holding or soft kisses.

As they continued their walk to the bus stop they almost passed by the dancing couple. Kwame spotted them first.

"Damn! Look at them two old women dancing over there." He shouted.

"They old as my momma!" He sauntered up to the dancing couple.

"Back that ass up!" He laughed, capering around the dancing lovers.

Ignoring the teenagers, smiling slightly, the couple continued to dance, moving to music only they could hear, looking deeply and lovingly into one another's eyes.

Kwame and Imani stood silently, staring at the dancers. They had never seen dancing like this, so different from the sexual gyrations they had grown up watching.

The dancers swayed, soulfully, doing a little dip now and then. Almost despite themselves Imani and Kwame moved closer together, their hands brushing together. This dancing touched them and moved them in ways that the overt sexuality of their favorite rap stars never had.

Just then, one of the women reached up and stroked the cheek of the other. Imani thought of all the times she had wanted to touch Kwame like that. She thought about how beautiful she thought his strong black face was as he moved over her during sex or concentrated over a calculus problem.

Kwame continued to silently watch the women dance. He focused on their faces, on how their eyes never left the others. He knew he wanted to look at Imani like that, sometimes, but thought she would think he was weak, a punk. He thought about all the things he wanted to share with Imani. How he wanted to tell her how beautiful she looked on the stage during the Black History Month assembly last year, how he loved her sweet voice and how smart he thought she was. How proud of her he was when she got her acceptance letter to Spellman.

Slowly, Kwame moved closer to Imani. Hesitantly he took her hand in his and turning her face to his, he looked into her eyes and they began to dance underneath the sparkling lights of the hotel's holiday display. Softly crooning love songs they didn't know they knew.

The parking lot was crowded as Grace and Malcolm entered. Their voices were strident as they continued the argument about the movie they had seen.

"I just don't know why the brother had to be so gay, so flaming." Said Malcolm.

"I thought he was sweet. He kind of reminded me of your old boo—the one I met that time at the Pan African Film Festival." Grace whispered.

"Where are Faith and Medgar?" Malcolm said, tapping his foot impatiently, "It's cold out here."

Just then Faith came walking up, Medgar not far behind. "Ya'll hungry?" She asked.

"Starvin!" The three friends said in sync. "Sounds like a Roscoe's night to me." Said Faith with a grin, thinking about her favorite spot.

The restaurant was crowded as the foursome arrived. The air was full with the scents of sweet maple syrup, spicy fried chicken and good, hot coffee. Putting their names on the list they then went to sit in the front waiting area. Faith noticed the dancing couple first.

"Will you look at that" she hissed, hitting Grace on the thigh.

Underneath the parking lot lights, the couple danced, swaying softly and crooning old-fashioned love songs. It was as if they were in another world. Ignoring the coming and going cars, the late night partiers, the busy street sounds; they danced. Occasionally dipping and twirling, laughing softly at one another; they danced.

"Oh, how sweet." Grace crooned, unconsciously moving closer to Faith who was sitting next to her on the waiting area bench.

"They need to take that stuff home!" Faith snapped, moving away from Grace and looking uncomfortably around.

The taller woman was dressed in a dashiki made of Kente clothe, while the smaller one had on a skirt in bright reds, greens and black. Though far from young they moved with grace and ease and there was something innocent in the way they through back their heads and laughed at their whispered jokes and comments.

The four friends watched silently, each lost in their own thoughts. Medgar was remembering the time when he used to feel as free and authentic as the dancing women. Recalling how that began to change as he entered this relationship, with all its rules and boundaries.

The couple continued to dance, moving to music only they could hear, looking deeply and lovingly into one another's eyes.

Grace was wondering what it would feel like to dance so freely in the arms of her loved one. Dancing with abandon, not caring what the world thought. Dancing and moving in love, with love, for love.

Faith was so uncomfortable, frightened for the two women. What if someone they know sees them? She thought. What if some asshole tries to hurt them because of who they are?

Malcolm, deep in thought, felt his eyes began to tear as he thought about what it must feel like to be so in love that you believed the world was your dance floor. How big that kind of love could be, how scary, how intense, how utterly real and present and brave you had to be to love like that.

The four friends continued to watch the twirling, dipping, gliding couple. They had been friends for so long, and had held each other's secrets for so long they some times forgot reality. They never discussed the nature of their relationship, preferring to leave much undefined and unsaid.

Their deception began many years ago on a Christmas day. Malcolm's family had been nagging him all that year about when was he going to get serious about a woman. Medgar, who had long ago distanced himself from his family, was tired of staying home, alone, on major holidays. They were arguing about what they were going to do when Faith, their neighbor from upstairs, knocked on the door.

"Hey guys, I was wondering if I could borrow a cup of sugar, I don't have quite enough for the sweet potato pies I'm making." She said, peeking into the immaculate apartment.

"Sure" said Malcolm, heading for the kitchen "I'll get it for you."

Medgar smiled shyly at the woman who had moved in so recently. He thought she might be family, but wasn't sure how to find out without offending her. "Do you have plans for the day?" he asked.

"Not really" she sighed "My friend, Grace, might come by later but she's spending most of the day with her family. My people are from the Islands and its just too far and expensive to go.

"I thought I heard a slight accent." Said Malcolm, walking back in with the sugar. "Where are your people from?"

"Barbados, but I've been here a long time. Thought I lost my accent." She laughed softly.

164

"Hey, Faith." Said Malcolm. "Why don't you join us at my family's house today. I'm sure they'd love to have you and it would make things a little easier for Medgar and me."

Faith started to ask for an explanation but then thought better of it. "Sure, I'd love to." She said, feeling relieved at not having to spend the holiday alone.

At Malcolm's parent's home, later that day, it just seemed easier to let everyone make their own conclusions. When Malcolm's sister, Winnie, asked how long Faith had been seeing Malcolm, Faith shrugged, glanced quickly at Medgar and said "A while."

When Grace moved in with Faith a couple of months later, the two couples began to spend more and more time together. They found they had much in common, especially their love of art movies, Ethiopian food and open air jazz concerts. The two women felt safer in the company of the two strong handsome young brothers and the men, although never admitting it, felt safer too.

Grace invited Faith, Medgar and Malcolm to the company dinner when she received the employee of the year award. When she introduced them to her co-workers she just let everyone assume that Malcolm was her man and that Grace and Medgar were together. The next day at work she never corrected the teasing she received about her 'fine man'.

The closet they lived in was roomy, comfortable enough that only occasionally did they question it. Medgar sometimes wished for the ease of previous relationships with brothers who were much more 'out'. He waxed nostalgic about the days when he proudly walked, arm in arm, with whatever beautiful black man he was dating. But he loved Malcolm and was willing to sacrifice for their relationship.

He still remembered Malcolm's pain the night he lay sobbing in Medgar's arms after Malcolm's father, speaking of a distant cousin, said that the cousin's AIDS was a "curse from God for his sissy ass."

The fact that they really enjoyed and came to love one another made the secrets they shared and the lies that they told more palatable. But there was a price to pay, Faith, reflected as they watched the dancing couple. The price of not being able to look, in public, with love upon your beloved's face seemed a very high cost.

The women continued to dance, their softly murmured loved songs lilted on the night air. Faith leaned over to Grace, "I love you." She said softly, tentatively.

Grace drew her breath in sharply and took a quick, worried look around the waiting area. What she saw stunned her, deeply. All the other waiting patrons were watching the dancing couple too. But instead of the looks of disgust or discomfort that she expected to see, there were looks of envy, of admiration, of longing and of joy. Joy for the two beautiful souls whose every movement spoke of a deep and true and endless love.

Breathing in deeply, Grace leaned over to Faith. "I love you, too, Baby." She said, not in a whisper but in a strong, clear voice. Taking Faith's hand she led her to the parking lot. The dancing couple paused a moment, bowed slightly, smiled fondly at the younger women and resumed their dance. Grace and Faith joined them, dipping, twirling swaying and then laughing out loud as Malcolm and

Medgar walked up, locked in embrace, and began to dance, softly crooning love songs they didn't know they knew.

Nia jumped up and down, excitedly as she waited for her mom to come up the apartment stairs. "Can we go to the park now?" she cried before her mother could get into the cramped apartment.

Miss Rhodesa, the kindly woman from down the hall, shook her head at the child's enthusiasm. "I told her you had to work late and probably couldn't take her to the park tonight."

Trying to shake off the tiredness in her bones, Cheryl smiled at the excited four-year old. "Baby, can it wait until tomorrow?"

"You promised, Mommie!" Nia said, tears starting to well up in her enormous brown eyes.

"Yes, Baby, I promised, and a promise is a promise. But we can't stay too late, its already getting dark." Cheryl sighed as she pulled back on the sweater she had started to take off. Pulling her thick braids through, she gave her head a slight shake. Nia asks for so little, she thought, how can I disappoint her again?

As Nia skipped and hopped down the narrow sidewalk, Cheryl was lost in thought, remembering all the disappointments she and her beloved child had already suffered. The Christmas and birthday presents that Kenny promised and never sent, the phone calls that never came, the child support payments that were always behind and never for the correct amount. She recalled the time she had gotten Nia all dressed up, bright and early, for Kenny's promised trip to the zoo. How Nia had waited on the stoop all that morning, looking right then left then right again for her dad's old, red Mazda to pull her. Her sobs when Cheryl tried to get her to come back inside. The phone call from Kenny that didn't come until the next day, saying sheepishly that something had 'come up'.

As they neared the park, Nia's excitement grew. "Look, Mommie, I can see the swings and I think there is a new monkey bar." Her beautiful cocoa colored face glowed beneath her neatly parted cornrows.

Cheryl was grateful to see the city had repaired the broken lights and that the park looked safe and clean that night. Living in a crowded one- room apartment was hard on Nia and the busy street in front of their place was not safe for a child to play. The only time Nia got to run, jump and climb was on these evening trips to the park. She looked on fondly, as Nia began to climb up the stairs to her favorite slide.

Taking her seat on the bench that she knew would provide her with the best view of Nia's antics, she saw the two women dancing. It surprised her to see the two middle-aged women in the park at night. Except for the young men who nightly claimed the basketball courts she and Nia were usually the park's only nighttime visitors. The two women were dancing under the newly repaired lights, undulating gently in time to music, that although Cheryl strained her ears, she could not hear. Cheryl thought perhaps she had seen the women before, perhaps at the local farmer's market or maybe at the community rally she had attended against police brutality. What beautiful black women, she thought, and then with a sigh, how I miss my mama. Mama would be about their age, now, and I bet she would have loved to dress up in those fabulous mud cloth coats they have on.

The couple continued to dance, moving to music only they could hear, looking deeply and lovingly into one another's eyes. Cheryl was so lost in thought, in her enjoyment of the beauty of the two women that she didn't hear the soft footsteps of the solidly built young man as he walked up behind her. Leaning over he whispered in her ear, "Hey, Baby."

"Kenny!" Cheryl exclaimed, jumping up from her seat, "What are you doing here?"

"Miss Rhodesa told me you guys come down here every evening when you get home. I thought maybe we could go grab a bite to eat when Nia gets thru playing."

"Kenny, we haven't seen you for almost two months and now you just want to come back with no explanation, nothing......just lets grab a bite to eat!!" Cheryl's soft voice couldn't hide the anger she felt.

"Not this time, Kenny, no way!"

Kenny sat quietly, letting Cheryl's indignant words wash over him. He knew she was right. How could he make her see he was different now, ready to be a real husband to her and a real father to Nia.

"Cheryl," Kenny said quietly, "I need to talk to you about something that happened to me. Last month I got a phone call from my dad. Now, you know I hadn't seen nor heard from my dad since he left my mom and me when I was 10. And I wasn't tryin' to hear from him when he called. Matter of fact, I hung the phone up the first two times he called. On the third time I let it go to voice mail.

169

Cheryl, he left me a message sayin' he was sick, real sick and could I come see him."

Cheryl sat quietly, listening, her eyes moving back and forth from Kenny's tired, anxious face to Nia who was still engrossed in her adventures on the slide and monkey bars. Occasionally her eyes would drift over to the two dancing women. She thought they might be quietly watching her and Kenny. Something in their glances reminded her of the way her mama always kept one eye on her, even when she was a young woman pregnant with Nia. Watching, to be sure no harm would come to her, as if her watching could make Kenny do right by her.

Kenny kept talking, softly, looking imploringly into Cheryl's face. "I went to see him, Cheryl. It was bad. He was in the hospital and barely knew me. He had two other kids there, too. We all looked alike and none of them seem to know my dad any better than I did. I hadn't even been there a whole day when he passed away. The doctors said there was nothing they could do."

Despite herself, Cheryl began to soften. Her hand reached up and gently touched Kenny's face. "I'm sorry, so sorry." She whispered.

Kenny began to speak again. Cheryl's touch seemed to strengthen him. "It all made me think, baby. I don't want Nia to ever have to say good-bye to a daddy she didn't even know. I want to be a real father to her and if you'll let, me a real man to you. I promise I'll spend the rest of my life working to make you and Nia safe and happy."

Cheryl's tears began to fall delicately down her mahogany cheeks. She sat perfectly still, her lips moving in silent prayer. "God, please don't let this man hurt me again, show me, ancestors, what should I do?"

Just then Kenny became aware of the dancing women.

He inhaled and said, "How beautiful! How perfect they look." The women seemed to hear his soft words. Smiling softly, they bowed slightly to the young couple, offering a benediction of sorts.

Just then Nia looked over to her mother's bench and spotted her father. "Daddy! Daddy!" Her short, stocky legs ran as fast as they could across the asphalt. Jumping into his lap, she buried her head in his broad chest. "I knew you would come. I prayed and asked God to send you home and I just knew She would."

Kenny sat holding Nia, looking across the playground at the dancing women. Cheryl continued to pray, knowing that she was at a turning point in her life and most importantly in Nia's life.

Looking again at the dancing women, at once a feeling of peace and certainty came over her. This is my life, she thought, loving and being loved, risking everything for love. This is what I am here for.

Rising gracefully, she urged Kenny to his feet. Encircling Nia they began to dance, moving gracefully as if they shared one body. Softly crooning love songs they didn't know they knew.

The airport was crowded, people waiting for family members, business associates, lovers. The terminal was abuzz with a multitude of languages. Swahili, the soft click of the Xosa. The melodic Zula. A sprinkling of Bemba,

Bantu and Yoruba. There was color everywhere. Bright Kente clothe pant suits, embroidered dashikis in every color of the rainbow, tribal patterned long skirts swaying gently on the ample hips of the women. The air was alive with smells. Spicy foods, fresh fruits and sweet drinks all combined for an indescribably delicious aroma.

The beautiful, stately black woman waited anxiously for the plane that was several hours late. She was magnificently tall with a broad, solid back and ample behind. Her softly graying locks were standing out all over her head, defying gravity. It was her eyes and her smile that people noticed most. Despite her obvious anxiety her dark brown eyes were kind and gentle with a shining intelligence and wit. She smiled at all who passed by, a smiled that beckoned, that said be well, be happy. Several children in the terminal were drawn to that smile. They came shyly up to her, extending an offering of some treat to share or a treasure to show.

One little girl watched quietly for a long while. She had no offering with which to break the ice. She was thin, her skin dark and shiny; her clothes shabby but very clean. Her thick black hair was neatly plated in three fat braids. The older woman watching her seemed exhausted, barely able to keep her eyes open.

Finally, seeing a break in the throng of children around the beautiful woman the little girl approached.

"You waiting on a plane from 'Merica too? She asked shyly

"Yes," the woman said gently "It's hard waiting so long isn't it?"

"My mama sister on that plane. She a big girl, not little like me. She been going to college in 'Merica and now she's coming home. Granny says she's gonna be a doctor and help a lotta people."

"How nice." Smiled the woman. "Your granny must be very proud."

"Uh huh. Granny says she's proud of *all* her girls. The ones livin' and the ones not livin'. My mama she's one of the not livin' ones but Granny says that's okay 'cause she watches over me from Heaven. Granny says I have to make my mama proud just like she made her mama proud." The words spilled out of the child, so grateful to have an interested listener that she forgot her shyness.

"Granny says that no matter what anyone says she is proud of *all* her daughters. She says I gotta be proud too and when people ask me about my mama I just gotta tell em: she's passed on, that she got AIDS and she had to go to heaven 'cause it got to hard for her to stay here and fight. Granny says we gotta *talk* about AIDS that we gotta educate us about it. Do you know about AIDS?" the child sternly asked the beautiful woman.

"Why don't you tell me about it?' the woman kindly asked.

"Okay, look; the A is for acquired, acquired means you can get it from somewhere and if you can get it then Granny says that means you can protect yourself so that you don't get it." As the child went on sharing proudly what she had been taught about AIDS the beautiful woman allowed her mind to wander a bit, smiling encouragement from time to time at the child.

What is taking that plane so long, she thought with mounting impatience. I've waited so long for this moment, I've dreamed about this for so many nights.

"Busi! Busi! Where are you child? Come quick!" the grandmother called.

"She's here! Oh, she's here! Look Madam my auntie is getting off the plane!"

The beautiful woman watched as the lovely, dark young woman got off the plane. She was simply an older, more poised version of the little girl. The child and her grandmother both were dancing with an excitement they could not contain. As the young woman reached them they joined in a big, tearful hug. The beautiful woman watched silently, tears streaming down her face, her heart filled hope and love for her people. The little girl turned once to wave as the family walked off.

The overhead speakers continued to blare announcements of arriving and departing flights. But not the much anticipated one. The beautiful woman, dosed occasionally. Her dreams were of her loved one, of all the happy times they had shared together, of all the plans they had for the future.

The soft, excited chattering of the 2 women nearby woke her. They were middle aged, comfortable looking women. They were dressed in soft, comfortable sweat suits, trimmed in Kente cloth. The smaller one had long, graying locks almost touching her behind. The plumper one had a freshly cut short afro that perfectly framed her elegant head.

9.3 Tips for success

As you work your way through the 30-day intermittent fasting program, here are a few tips to helpyou stay on track and achieve success:

• Plan your meals: It can be helpful to plan out your meals in advance to make sure you aregetting enough nourishment during your eating window. This can also help you avoid thetemptation to reach for unhealthy foods when you are feeling hungry.

• Don't skip meals: It's important to eat during your eating window, even if you are not feelingparticularly hungry. Skipping meals can make it harder to stick to your fasting schedule and may cause you to feel weak or sluggish.

• Listen to your body: Intermittent fasting is not right for everyone, and it's important to listento your body and pay attention to how you are feeling. If you are feeling excessively hungryor tired, or if you are experiencing any other negative side effects, it may be necessary toadjust your fasting schedule or consider a different approach to weight loss and health.

• Stay active: Exercise can be a great way to boost weight loss and improve overall healthwhile intermittent fasting. Try to incorporate some form of physical activity into your daily routine, whether it's a brisk walk, a yoga class, or a high-intensity interval training (HIIT)

workout. Just be sure to listen to your body and don't push yourself too hard, especially ifyou are new to exercise or have any underlying health conditions.

Don't get discouraged: Intermittent fasting can be challenging at times, and it's normal to have setbacks or moments of temptation. If you slip up or have a less-than-perfect day, don't get discouraged. Just get back on track and keep going. Remember, the key to success with intermittent fasting is consistency.

9.4 Troubleshooting Common Issues with Intermittent Fasting

While intermittent fasting can be an effective and beneficial eating pattern, it's not without its challenges. Here are some common issues that may arise and how to troubleshoot them:

• Hunger: It's normal to feel hungry during the fasting periods, especially at first. If you are struggling with hunger, try drinking plenty of water, eating filling and nourishing foods during your eating window, and engaging in physical activity to help reduce hunger pangs. You may also want to consider gradually increasing your fasting period over time to help your body adjust.

• Low energy: If you are feeling weak or sluggish while intermittent fasting, it may be due to low blood sugar or insufficient calorie intake. Try eating more balanced meals during your eating window and incorporating more healthy fats and proteins to help keep your energy levels stable.

• Difficulty sticking to the plan: It can be tough to stick to any new eating pattern, and intermittent fasting is no exception. If you are having difficulty sticking to your fasting schedule, try to identify

"No ma'am, I'm a right. My husband will be right back, he went to get me a cup of tea." The young woman said, softly.

"You have a husband considerate enough to get you a cup of tea and yet you are crying as if your heart is broken, why?" asked the beautiful woman.

The young woman began to cry all the harder. Between sobs she told a familiar story. A story of dreams for a better life and no employment opportunities. A story of hopes for a chance in America to create that dreamed of better life. A story of the realization that only one of them could make the trip at this time, and a story of the possibility of several years of separation.

"It's just all so hard." Wailed the young woman. "We've only been married one year and now this."

"I know, I know." Consoled the beautiful woman "But you can do it, I know you can. Be strong, God will be with you."

"Tell me your name." Said the beautiful woman. "I will keep you in my prayers."

"Oh thank you so much, I'm Shola and please prayer for my husband, Malik, also. The beautiful woman watched as Shola's young husband returned to her with a cup of tea. Enfolding her gently in his arms her tenderly kissed the top of her head while she slowly drank her tea. Offering up a silent affirmation for the young couple the beautiful woman moved on.

As she continued her stroll through the terminal she reflected upon the difficulties of the past two years.

Leaving her loved one had been the most difficult day of her life. The odyssey that followed had not been without hardships but none that compared to the day that they parted.

Manifesting your dream is never easy, she thought, but nothing is more worthwhile. Being of service to African people, bearing witness to the struggles and pain of her people had been even more miraculous than she had imaged. The friendships she had made, the sharing of the daily joys and triumphs of village life were such a wonderful and unexpected gift. I've created a home for her, she mused, a place of simple beauty and warmth; a place where we can spend the rest of our days. She smiled, thinking of the surprises that awaited her baby, the beautiful altar, awash in the power and beauty of feminine deity; the chair carved with love and a natural skill; and of course, their marriage bed with the brightly colored African quilt. Lost in these thoughts she moved through the terminal, unaware of all the people who stopped to admire her quiet grace and bold beauty.

Glancing up, from a distance she could see a small figure, dressed all in white. It can't be she thought, they said gate 7. She moved forward quickly. She couldn't take her eyes off of the hurrying figure. It is her, it is, she thought breaking out into a run.

People moved out of the way, staring at the two figures as they seemed to fly towards one another. Reaching each other the smaller woman leapt into the beautiful woman's arms.

"Baby, baby, baby." They crooned to one another.

"Beloved." They whispered.

"Thank you God." They reverently prayed.

Slowing, gracefully the two woman began to dance together. Dancing as if they had never been apart. Moving and swaying together as if their bodies were one. As they twirled and dipped and glided people stopped to watch in awe.

Mothers hugged their babies tenderly. Lovers moved closer together, locking hands or arms. Strangers stopped to smile at one another, making eye contact that said hello my brother or sister.

The elderly newspaper man was the first to join in the dance, taking the hand of the pretty young ticket agent he began to lead her with surprising agility and grace. Soon everyone in the terminal was dancing. As the beautiful woman and her loved one spun through the crowds they could see Busi laughing and twirling in the arms of her beloved auntie.

Whole families were dancing, in big circles, laughing uproariously. Billie and Simone were just standing and swaying gently side to side while their sons strutted and stepped to ancient rhythms.

Young lovers invited the single travelers to join in their embraces. Mothers were dancing with daughters, fathers with sons. The group of teenagers lost some of their awkwardness and began to dance with each other in couples and threesomes. One student began to dance with the teacher, her face shining with pleasure. The beautiful woman smiled at Busi and Malik, dancing with a strength and assurance that said we *can* do this.

People were dancing everywhere, the old, the young, the tired, the energized, the well off and the poor. People were dancing with sacred and passionate joy. Powerful, marvelous, amazing, extraordinary, loving African people, softly crooning love songs they didn't know they knew.

C. Jerome Woods

MESHUGA: MALCOLM OR MARTIN
by C. Jerome Woods

Why do you act as if presenting a gift with
Words so unkind.

You speak with gnawing teeth, twisted tongue;
As if it and your face are fresh out of my behind.

Words so unkind.

You rant with the N-word, fag, terrorist, and Jew. How unrefined.
Watch your mouth and back. You must be outta' yo (more French)
mind!

Words so unkind.

Books, degrees, tenure, privilege have not taught you a thing.
Ignorance and insecurities show. Your opinion of others will not have
freedom ring.

Words so unkind.

You apathetic semblance of a man. I hope my posture.....my presence
sting.
Don't mess with me. You betta' get ta steppin'. I'm not Martin Luther
King.

Word!

THE ONE

by C. Jerome Woods

Buzios, thrown, Ifa', orixa, home goings, Sankofa in flight.
Most beautiful pearl, the deepest of night.

Special evenings of glass raised champagne toasts.
The midnight baby enchanted.

The "to die for" business, cocktail or evening dress.
Dark continent bearing all homo-sapiens.

The pride sang by James Brown and orated by Booker T.
Place of Garvey's "Back To....Movement."

Color from which God brought creation.
The hinterland forest.

Texas tea erupting from golden undergrounds.
Syrup, honey-sweet and tongue tying.

The one who gave birth to civilizations, universities, mathematics,
Military might, astronomy, invention and humanity.

The ideal man in body and spirit.
Consummate purse, power or infinite recess in outer space.

The church, the corporation, the child.
Coal or diamond brilliance.

The giver of light and warmth.
Asphalt maps to Memphis, Mexico and Mecca.

Indians of New Orleans.
Rising complexions of Venezuela, revolutions in the Sudan.

The words of Countee cullen, Ma Rainey, Richard Wright, James
Baldwin, Essex Hemphill,

Fannie Lou Hamer, Alice Walker, Stanley Bennett Clay, Qevin Oji,
my mother.

The faces of Naomi Sims, Seal, Desmond Tutu, Marlon Riggs, Van
Der Zee, Dorothy Taylor's dolls,
Ron Jackson's jewelry, Lula Washington and Raymond Johnson's
"Ceremonies."

Aunt Rosa Lee's grits and sweet tea, Chef Marilyn's succotash and
Dulan's catering.
The D. C. caucus, Brian Breye's museum and CAAM.

Cajun fish, Gullah people, Caribbean islands, Cuban beans.
Roderick & Jacqueline Sykes' art, American culture, departmental
studies,
airplane boxes, Kosher coffee, altar offerings.

I am the one; that one.
The darkest berry with the sweetest juice.

I am the one.....the community......unity.
The raised, clenched fist of the 60s.

The one with twists, locks, dreads-coarse and fine.
Faces, noses; eyes divine.

I am the dual spirited ancestral guide.
Bearer of good news. Across astral waters, I glide.

I am the one; that one!

The Black one!

WHAT'S UP, MY BROTHER

by C. Jerome Woods

They walk amongst us

Wide stride

Smiling

Prepared, restricted, lurking

Young, older, prancing

Swaggin'

At attention

Calling none to themselves

Dressed and not

Arms folded

Claimed fingers holding; surrounding dark joe

Lukewarm lattes

Lascivious minds that mesh, meander

Assimilate, depending on time, temperature and temperament

Traffic

They arrive in Converse, Nike, patent leather, Kenneth Cole

Cardboard

Praising, positioning, perpetrating

Precious, patient

With probable cause

Larry, Johnny, Calvin, Cleo, Clint, Bob, Jamal

Representing one in the White House, One million in prison

Trendy, tiny, belts taut

Blackberry, flip, clip, Kindle

Politics in their pockets

Police injustices in their minds.

Habaragani, asalaam alaykum, Shalom, Axe'.

What's up?

My brotha!

Vigil For Brother Kato

Gathering at dusk
We come.
In awe
We come.
Not with good news of the day.
Nonetheless, we come.
Gathering at dusk.

We greet by candlelight.
In vigil because of a vile deed
We come.
Together
In Kente, mud cloth, denim, and linen
We gather at dusk
In star bright
We come
In handfuls and by the hundreds
With community.

We gather at dusk
And in candlelight
To mourn a murder
Celebrate a kindred spirit
Champion a cause
Challenge an unjust system
Stimulate minds.

We come to Leimert Park Village, the Shaw
We come from Xhosa highlands,
Egyptian hieroglyphics,
Ugandan huts, hollywood Hills,
Happy times, homelessness
Jamaican Maroon colonies.
Belezian hideaways

Coalitions and collaborations

We come in pieces; broken and fragile
We come as kin; peaceful, powerful, with pride
We come searching; for acknowledgment, recognition and grace
We come giving; resolve, hope, assurance
Tonight we come from secret places and sacred spaces
Vast savannahs, the Middle Passage
Out from the muddy Mississippi
Down the rough side of the mountain.....We fear no evil.

We are vigilant.
We have voice; We have say.
We hurt and heal
Shout and pray.
Lesbian, bisexual, transgender, heterosexual
Questioning, curious
Same Gender Loving, gay.
Visible, valued, youth, middle aged, elderly gray.
Seeking justice for David Kato and others along The Great Black
Way.
We are here to stay.

We build
We care
We love
We gather at dusk
By candlelight
And in the light of day.

(The ancestors and we say so......and so it is! Peace and presence
be with you as we continue in the struggle and as we continue to
unite. Axe', Axe', Axe'.)

The Editors of Tapestries of Faith

Ifalade Ta'Shia Asanti: Is an award-winning writer, poet, journalist, TV producer and filmmaker. The author of three books, Ta'Shia continues to pen fiction that she hopes will facilitate critical thinking in conjunction with what she calls, "juicy fiction." Recipient of the Audre Lorde Black Quill Award for Creating Positive Images of Black Women in the Arts, the award for Best Contemporary Fiction by a Woman of Color and the Urban Spectrum Media Award for Outstanding Achievement in the Field of Journalism, Ta'Shia's newest book delves into the very fabric of love and its richly diverse expressions. Also look for Ta'Shia's new Talk Show airing on Your World TV, The Window, which uses social commentary to explore the issues at the forefront of global culture. More about Ta'Shia's work can be found at www.tashiaasanti.com

Jeffrey King: Is the founder and Executive Director of In The Meantime Men, Inc. which is a 10 year old 501 (C) 3 non-profit community service organization. In The Meantime Men's Group, Inc. is purposed to enrich, empower, and extend the lives of intergenerational black men, respectful of sexual orientation, through social, educational, health and wellness programs and services. In The Meantime Men's Group provides HIV/AIDS education, and awareness trainings. Provide both group and individual peer and professional mental health counseling options for Black men. An open weekly social/ discussion group, an annual Black Men's empowerment retreat, an annual Black Men's Health Conference. Jeffrey's organization also provides a variety

of social/ community cultural events and activities for the Black LGBT community. More about Jeffrey King and his empowering organization can be found at www.inthemeantimemen.org

Azaan Kamau: Is an award winning nationally syndicated journalist, poet, photographer, book designer, entrepreneur and author of 14 books! Azaan's work has been included in a host of anthologies, publications, magazines and at the famous Getty Museum! Azaan has also been nominated for several awards! Azaan's publishing company Glover Lane Press is growing and expanding rapidly due to it's focus on socially conscious media. Glover Lane Press offers high quality publishing, book design, photography, and many other services. Azaan recently published the Inspirational *Got Homophobia!* Please visit Azaan at: www.gloverlanepress.webs.com or www.azaankamau.webs.com

AFTERWORD-AZAAN KAMAU

As a community of SGLBT African Americans, we have been wounded by a great many things. My family and close friends have been affected directly by the HIV/AIDS pandemic. What I learned from the pain is that we must empower ourselves with self-love, information, proactive decision making, and open community dialogue.

My beloved brother Dijan died from the complications of HIV/AIDS. I believe HIV/AIDS is condition of the spirit. Our young African American men who were made to feel ashamed, the tortured, neglected, bullied, molested, humiliated, ostracized, wounded, oppressed, and suppressed. These African American men are susceptible to this disease. Our SGLBT youth are at risk for HIV/AIDS, if they were taught they are not good enough, not worthy of love and that something is wrong with them!

I believe religious views, economic, and social barriers have increased the inequality in healthcare as it pertains to HIV/AIDS. For years there has been a stigma in our community that prohibited African Americans from obtaining accurate information on prevention and combating the disease.

I realize after the loss of my brother and our close friends that it is entirely up to us to confront and oppose these issues. We can prevent and stop this systematic destruction of our people. We must get involved and save the future of our SGLBT brother and sisters! People continually ask me, "what can I do, I'm just one person"? Well, you can start by volunteering at our SGLBT organizations that are fighting the war on AIDS. You can donate, write for a publication, or deliver a meal to a hospice. Engage your friends, family, church, etc. Get everyone you know involved.

This book of ultimate sacrifice, re-birth and healing is dedicated to Dijan Bruttus and the many who lost their fight as an SGLBT person.

In Loving Memory of

Dijan "Donnie" Bruttus

April 26, 1967-May 25ᵗ 2004

Obituary

Dijan "Donnie" Bruttus was born April 26, 1967 to Betty Bruttus in Los Angeles California. As a youth Dijan was gifted, artistic and quite talented. Dijan loved poetry, black & white photography, designing his own clothes, and most of all the art of dance. Dijan was charismatic, charming, and absolutely hilarious. He kept me laughing! Despite life's circumstances, Dijan grew into a caring passionate man who kindly helped strangers, protected people and gave his last dime to help someone. He was an extraordinary human being.

Dijan was a proud gay man! He became the epitome of SGLBT resistance in America. Dijan became involved in many SGLBT organizations, using himself as a tool to help others. Dijan absolutely loved *The Study,* an African American men's bar in Los Angeles where he felt safe and connected to his community.

On May 25ᵗʰ, 2004 Dijan Bruttus passed away from HIV/AIDS related renal failure. He was preceded in death by his mother Betty Bruttus and also his life-partner Jermaine Stewart. To cherish his beautiful memory, he leaves his siblings, several nieces, nephews and a host of friends who love him dearly.

May your humanly wounds heal as you rest eternally in peace my beloved angel.

Azaan Kamau, Desiree X & Family June 5, 2011

www.ingramcontent.com/pod-product-compliance
Lightning Source LLC
LaVergne TN
LVHW051233080426
835513LV00016B/1567